SELI

JOHN OF RUUSBROEC

SELECTED WORKS

OF

JOHN OF RUUSBROEC

WITH A NEW INTRODUCTION

BY

JAMES COWAN

Azafran Books

Translated from Flemish by C. A. Wynschenk

First published in 1916 by J.M. Dent & Sons

Published by Azafran Books –
http://www.azafranbooks.com/

ISBN-13: 978-1-9996600-0-0 (paperback)
First published in this edition: March 2018

Edited, formatted & design concept by Solomon James
Cover design & design concept by B.S.
John of Ruusbroec portrait by B.S.

Azafran Books
info@azafranbooks.com

CONTENTS

JOHN OF RUUSBROEC – HIS LIFE & WORK

Late medieval Europe was blessed with a number of important religious thinkers who enlivened the austere Aristotlism of past scholastic writers. Men such as Meister Eckhart, John Tauler, and mystics such as Julian of Norwich and Walter Hilton helped to leaven a Christianity that was in danger of becoming reduced to an arid analysis of dogma for its own sake. This new generation of writers, however, helped to breathe fresh life into a moribund system of belief that threatened to diminish Christ's importance for laymen and cleric alike. One of the most important of these thinkers of the fourteenth-century was John of Ruusbroec whose books, *The Sparkling Stone* and *The Book of Supreme Truth,* reflect a re-invigorated emphasis upon the works of Dionysius the Areopagite and Boethius from an earlier age, and their commitment to giving expression to the mystical life as a viable spiritual practice.

Some men are born into such a life, never doubting their vocation even as children. Ruusbroec was such a man. Born in 1293 in the tiny village of Ruusbroec, not far from Brussels, we know little of his early life other than that he was brought up by his mother. According to one chronicler, he was strong-willed, adventurous and insubordinate. At the same time he was afflicted by a strange restlessness, as if there was something forever on his mind. At eleven he ran away from home. In Brussels he sought out his uncle, John Hinckaert, a canon at the cathedral of St. Gudule, who took young Ruusbroec into his monastery of two in the shadow of the cathedral walls, where he lived with his friend, Francis von Coudenberg, practicing the ascetical life. Together, the three of them began a collective life as monastics. John's of Ruusbroec's spiritual education began early under the guidance of Hinckaert and his friend.

By 1343 the three men had left Brussels where they had conducted pastoral work, in a bid to set up a small hermitage in Groenendaal to the south. A number of other men joined them and, after local pressure directed towards them, they decided to accept the rule of St. Augustine in place of their less structured and more reclusive existence. Ruusbroec became the first prior, and his old friend Francis the first provost. At Groenendaal monastery, Ruusbroec continued his lifelong practice of writing mystical treatises, which he had begun to write in Brussels. His reputation grew. Men of like mind such as Geert Grote (1340-1384) and another great mystical thinker already alluded to, John Tauler (1300-1361), who both figured in the growth of the Modern Devotion movement in Germany and the Netherlands, visited their Brabantine retreat for spiritual guidance and council. Often, even in old age, Ruusbroec would set out on long walks from Groenendaal to council people in their spiritual life. He died peacefully in December 1381 surrounded by his brethren.

The priory of Groenendaal lay in a forest. For John of Ruusbroec it was a perfect place to refine his devotions and cultivate his inner life. Other than when hunters came to the gates asking for food or a bed for the night, the priory enjoyed its silence. It is said that the trees became Ruusbroec's friends. He spent many hours among them, and often recited his treatises to a scribe while sitting by a tree trunk. His biographer records how he was discovered by one of the brothers seated under a tree, rapt in ecstasy, surrounded by an 'aura of radiant light.' The fruit of his meditations, it seems, thrived upon the interaction between himself and the woods.

A simple life, a peaceful death. These facts sum up the uneventful nature of John's life. If it were not for his many treatises he might well have escaped our notice. Yet he was no ordinary man. He lived at a time when much of Europe was experiencing a terrible pestilence, the spread of the bubonic plague. The disease had arrived in the Brabantine region around 1348 to begin its deadly decimation of agricultural communities, as well as its cities. By the late fourteenth century plague victims were already being depicted in illuminated manuscripts, asking for protection from their bishops. Half of the population of Paris (100,000), for example, died from the plague. To combat its effects, people resorted to astrology or the killing of Jews. The pandemic had reduced people to fear and loathing, to a sense that God was angry with their dissolute ways. Carts filled with bodies became a normal occurrence of a morning as these were being taken away for mass burial.

John's writings give no sense of any crisis near at hand, however. It was as if the world beyond the forest did not exist, at least not in his immediate thoughts. He attended mass, he meditated and he wrote. He became, in his own words, a ghostly man. Moreover, in his writings, he forsook Latin to write in his native Flemish, a genuine departure. Like Francis of Assisi, Jacapone di Todi, and Richard Rolle before him, the people's speech became his mode of communication. Vernacular not literary language was to be his vehicle of choice from hereon. Moreover, he realized that the old forms of literary structure could no longer contain the sublimity of his thought. He had to find another way of expressing himself. Images, not explanations, became the new order of the day for him, in spite of his ambivalence towards them. In using these as the substrate of his thought, he wrote, 'this green valley, the humble heart…becomes brighter and more illuminated.'

From this point onward, we find ourselves in a northern forest. Ruusbroec's mystical mind has become an extension to trees, to the fields, to nature itself. As he later wrote:

Pay attention to the wise bee, which gathers in the unity of its society and travels forth. Not in storms but in still, quiet weather and in sunshine, in order to visit all the blossoms where sweetness can be found. It never rests on any blossom, nor on any beauty or sweetness for very long. There it extracts from the bloom honey and wax – that is, the very sweetness and matter of illumination. Then the bee brings back what it has gathered to the assembled unity of other bees so that they might become fruitful…. The wise person should be as a bee, and fly with attention and with reason… and so taste the multiplicity of all consolation and goodness.

These are clearly the words of an observant man who loves the outdoors, and who sees nature as his book. For him, sapiential knowledge lies in a field of flowers or a babbling brook. He allows nature to teach him how to fashion correspondences that help him to bridge the gap between nature's innate wisdom and his own attempts at detailing the mystical impressions that he experiences.

Let us, then, gather for a brief moment in the forecourt of his thought. Here is a man who allowed the 'bright sun' of Christ to enliven the 'dawn' of his mother, Mary. The loveable sun of Christ 'flashed and shone yet brighter' with the fullness of all grace and all gifts. Moreover, Jesus was also the 'spotless lily and the common field flower' from which, supposedly, honey is drawn forth in order to bestow its sweetness. Christ is also a 'simple light' that penetrates a person, steadying him and helping him to sustain an inward unity of spirit and mind, by presenting himself as an avataric presence in his, John's, life.

John's dilemma is how to reconcile his understanding of the unity of deity on the one hand, with the natural multiplicity derived from manifestation on the other. By attempting to resolve this polarity at a mystical level, he is then able to declare what happens, inwardly, to a person who has made peace with such a dichotomy. 'A man is lifted up into a new state, and he turns inwards and focuses his memory on bareness, above all eruptions of sensible images, and above multiplicity,' he wrote in the *Espousals.* Here we see John struggling to *give up* his dependence upon images, in all their multiplicity, in his dogged pursuit of a supernatural inclination towards unity. Influenced as he is by Dionysius of Areopagite's negative theology – that is, towards eliminating any statement about what *is* – John of Ruusbroec finds himself exploring the concept of bareness and denudation of the sensible image. For a moment, it seems, flowers and trees and bees have become an impediment to laying bare what he calls the 'incomprehensible richness and sublimity, the outflowing, generous, and unique commonness of the divine nature.' Only this fact, this richness and sublimity of the divine nature, however, when it is clothed in images, can lead a person towards what he asserts is a state of pure 'astonishment.' That is, a onefoldedness in its very multiplicity. Such a vision of unity in astonishment, John seems to be saying, opens the door to an ever-deeper vision of what lies beyond the perception of the image.

John is taking us on a journey towards a 'one-fold clarity' where time and space no longer exist. Motion and change are suspended. Such a clarity stands outside the capacity of the faculties to give it form. The essence of the soul has become a spiritual kingdom filled with divine clarity. Only an understanding of onefoldedness can begin to make comprehensible the unity of our spirit with the supra-essential unity of the Divine. John is struggling now, and we can feel it. He has proposed the existence of a 'one-fold' nature which he sees as a form of eternal complacency, none other than a passivity in the presence of deity, which leads to a fathomless love of Being. Once more we find ourselves in the domain of antithesis and the need to reconcile polarities, which is the final resort of a mystical thinker.

Where else can one go? Beyond the metaphor, John seems to be saying, even though he himself was forced to use them often in his work. He is subject to a ghostly wound, a wound that he knows resides in his soul. Yet this wound pens the way for oneness to streams into his heart, in spite of the pain it causes. Only then can the 'quotidian fever' of multiplicity be neutralized. The dazzling splendor of the image must somehow be overcome. Even the faculty for making them in the first place must be put aside. What was once an 'unspotted lily amidst the flowers of the field' must be torn up by its roots from the imagination. John is looking for the abyssal and unconditioned Good which would otherwise be reduced, or clouded by images. In the end, he has to admit defeat. 'We must use sensible images,' he cries out at last, 'diverse similitudes and images.' Only these can give shape to differentiation, he finally admits, which is the final preserve of Godhead even in Its onefoldedness. John of Ruusbroec has been brought down to earth by his need to articulate divine absence with the only tool at his disposal, his imaginal intellect.

I try to walk in the woods with John and see what he sees. There are pine cones, lichens, flowers, broken boughs and fungus growing on tree trunks. There are feathers from birds, the skeletons of insects, nests in trees. These are what he sees; they are ordinary things, the repost of the earth going through the motions of stability and growth all at once. How can he extract from simple things a transcendent landscape? I ask myself this question because I want to know how to manipulate the sensible image into the making of what he calls a 'supernal stillness.' This is a condition that stands above all creatures, and yet infuses them at the same time. The reflexive nature of divinity, in that it eludes conceptual analysis, yet finds a way to dally among things, is key to John of Ruusbroec's mystical way of thinking.

At one point he speaks of Christ's touch. This touch invites our spirit to explore the most inward practices in order to emulate 'in a creaturely way' the created light that is Christ in his humanity. The spirit, through the power of love, raises itself above all works, 'into the unity where this life-giving spring or touch, gushes forth.' Such a touch, according to John, invites a man to know God in 'His brightness.' So God abides alone in his inborn radiance. Those who have pierced through 'their ground,' to their very source by way of inward practices, they alone are able to feel Christ's touch and thus 'see' His Light. When a person has felt His touch, then in Him 'love goes forward, while understanding stays outside.' John is asking us to believe that understanding is not fruition, that fruition lies more in 'tasting and feeling' than in understanding. At once we begin to know: the faculties have their limit, but are necessary for allowing the depth of divine love to come to rest 'inside' understanding itself.

John further maintains that all our senses become involved. Touch, for example, delivers empathy, not craving, to the hungry man. In the *Espousals* he elaborates what he means:

> God's touch and His gifts, our loving craving and our giving in return, keep love steadfast. This flowing-out and flowing-back causes the fountain of love to overflow. Thus God's touch and our love's craving become one single love. Here a person is so possessed by love that he must forget himself *and God* (our ital.), for he knows nothing but love. The spirit is burned up in the fire of love, and it goes so deeply into God's touch that it is overcome by all its craving, and it is reduced to nothing in all its acts.

It seems that God's touch embodies a simple act of amnesia: to forget It even as It forges a relationship with man. Inner practice is about forgetting all contingencies as it charts a course towards 'His fathomless love,' the one-foldedness of his divine nature. All of this allows John to see primal Reality, or deity itself, bearing a two-fold character, of the one and the many. Though it must be said that for a mystic like himself, its realization is partly a synthetic experience: it must be through thought analyzed in a particular mystical way, if it is ever to be grasped. God, as known by man, exhibits in Its perfection in these dual properties of Love - that is, the one and the many - while at the same time It continues to be active, generative, and creative.

Such a melding of duality and unity for John becomes an ineffable possession, which he calls a *Fruition.* It is one of Ruusbroec's master-words. God is, then, the Absolute One in whom the antithesis of Time and Eternity, of Being and Becoming, are finally resolved. God transcends the storm of succession, yet at the same time is the inspiration behind flux itself. According to his fruitional nature, God works without ceasing, for 'He is pure act.' He is the omnipotent and ever active creator of all things, an immeasurable 'Flame of Love' perpetually breathing forth energetic life in new births of being and new floods of grace. Thus the world of nature, none other than John's beloved trees, participate in this fruitional encounter with deity.

What makes a man bury himself in language in such a remarkable way, one might ask? What makes him put aside rapture in order to render it as words? I confess that I am shaken by his intensity of expression when it is raised to such fever pitch. I try to imagine what it must have been like for John to live his secluded life at Groenendaal, attending to his duties as a prior, yet ever able to explode with such mystical fervor when alone.

A single fathomless word he hears, and nothing more. Yet it is this word, he knows, that God uses to utter Himself without intermediary and without cease. The word, John contends, is the verb 'to see'. And this 'seeing' embodies the going-out as well as the advent of Christ as a beam of 'eternal light' directed towards him. Seeing becomes the birth of a rusticated love in the forest determined by nature as visionary cohort. Being seen in such a way, John himself becomes an enormous eye, a cosmic eye, ranging across the entire earth. Moreover, his eyes become as changeable as mercury in a bowl, an intense yet malleable presence confronting the enormity of the cosmos. He is enthralled. Finally he begins to perceive the inner activity of Being itself.

The first point and foundation of all spiritual life is to enter a state of 'bare imageless being,' says John in his masterpiece, *The Sparkling Stone.* Only then can one become a ghostly man. In doing so, one becomes effaced by the knowledge that in order to reach a point of 'indwelling and divine enjoyment,' it is necessary to understand the language of stone. Fundamentally, he believes, language is shaped out of silence. To be a mystic is to reach out to silence. And stones, for the most part, are silent. A mystic is always trying to formulate a language that is shaped by an un-articulated silence. As Apollodorus of Athens remarked, 'Silence honors the gods by imitating their nature, which is to escape meaning.' The mystic's task is therefore to find a way to escape meaning. He does so by entering that privileged place that is silence. The mystic, like the poet, has only two choices: either to look *at* things, or to *be* in them. Unlike the poet, the mystic invariably chooses the latter.

He feels the horizon of absence and unreality whenever he engages with rapture. In the course of his meditations he runs aground on the shore where he expected to arrive much later, that of his own annihilation. John must have known this feeling early in his vocation as a mystic. One senses that his retreat into the forest around Groenendaal was his way of managing the effects of his estrangement from things as that of being real. Clearly the stoniness or woodiness of things spoke to him. He listened to their individuation as things, their struggle to affirm existence by way of the non-conversation that he had with them. They were, so to speak, like steles or cicatrices, registering their 'marks' upon his consciousness. For him, language had become one of nature's hieroglyphs.

> I will give him a small sparkling stone, and in this stone a new name written which no one knoweth, except him who receiveth it. That stone is called a pebble, because it is so small that it will not hurt a man, even if he treads it underfoot. The small stone sparkles brightly, and it is red like a fiery flame. It is small and round and smooth and it is very light.

This is the way stones speak to John of Ruusbroec. The sparkling stone is none other than Jesus Christ. Why, one might ask? According to John, such a stone is known as a 'calculus', which is a small measuring stone used in computation. By extending his metaphors, he is able to suggest that this stone's smallness relates to that of Christ when he humbled himself, and allowed himself to die on the cross. 'I am a worm and not a man, the scorn of men and an outcast of the people.' Christ had made himself so small that Jews were able to tread on him - he, the sparkling stone of divine truth. Ruusbroec cannot put down the image; it fascinates him:

> The last feature of the stone I would like to speak of is that it is very light, for the Father's Eternal Word has no weight, and yet carries heaven and earth in its power. It is equally close to all things, and yet no man can overtake it, for it transcends all creatures. It takes precedence over them all. Moreover, it will release itself to those who it chooses, and where it chooses. Now its lightness, our heavy human nature, has gone beyond all the heavens, and sits crowned at the right hand of the father.

Contrasting 'heavy human nature' with the sparkling stone is one of John's verbal triumphs. Possessing the latter, that is, the sparkling stone, enables a man of contemplation to receive a new name, which is the door to living a mystical life. No one knows this secret name other than he upon whom it has been bestowed. This secret name of transcendence is a gift to all those who bear the tiny pebble of Christ in their innermost being.

Ruusbroec urges us to protect the stone within us if we wish to live a ghostly life:

> You must know that all spirits are given a name as they return to God, and each in accordance with the nobility of its service, and the high nature of its love.

The concept of waylessness, John later tells us, alluding of course to Christ as the Way, is the object or passage towards the mystical life, since only Christ has lived it. To pass into the presence of God, one must be wayless. It is the 'glorious wandering in the Super-essential Love wherein neither end nor beginning, nor way nor manner, can ever be realized.' For John this is a simple death-like passing, an annihilation of identity and ego. To be bare and wayless is to love consummately and without reserve. It is the perfect counterpoint to a life lived under the aegis of 'Reason and in Ways.' People who live in this "wayless way" become 'secret friends, the hidden sons of God.' Selfhood has been discarded like a worn-out coat. Then we are ready to gaze into our super-essence, and so receive, deep within us, a scintilla of God's essence in the form of our soul's growth. The 'deep quiet' of Godhead becomes a 'simple and abyssal tasting.' Living the God-seeing life, we feel ourselves to be living *in* God. From out of that life 'there shines forth on the inward face of our inward being a brightness that enlightens our reason as an intermediary between ourselves and God.'

Once more we are awash in the healing poultice of language. John of Ruusbroec is taking us to a place where few men have been. It is not so much a difficult place to find; rather, it is a place that is defined by the apophaticism of language itself, the pure negativity of words. It is as if words have the power to negate being, to be *without* being, and therefore owe nothing to being. To be released from being is the ultimate quest of the mystical thinker. He is free when he is released from his I-am-ness, and so denatured of his right to be. In him at this point the whole of humanity is embodied. The mystic stands within and above history at that moment in time.

Solitude becomes his companion, given that he exists outside normal contingencies. Free of being, so to speak, and separated *from* beings, the absolute I-am affirms itself in a supra-personal way, and without reference to others, except in a nominal way. In the process, a solitary holds himself back from nothingness, as did John of Ruusbroec. Through his waylesssness he found a way to negate being, yet allow it an existence that is both transcendent and real. As Holderlin remarked, one must preserve God through the purity of what distinguishes. Ruusbroec struggles with this challenge. He knows that his language is inadequate to that which he has witnessed under a tree in the forest. His rapture has become embroiled in the struggle to find adequate images to render it palpable to others.

To escape into non-being is the object of his quest. Non-being is a part of God, he knows that. Therefore he is trying to escape into God, as he feels himself drawn towards, and into Him, by His Love: '…for as long as we inwardly see that God wants to be ours, God's generosity will touch our greedy lust, and this causes restlessness of loving, for God's touch that flows out of us fans our restlessness and demands our action, namely that we love the love eternal.' 'And this touch that draws us inward makes us feel that God wants us to be His, for in it we must deny ourselves and allow Him to achieve *our* bliss. But where His touch flows out of us He leaves us to ourselves and makes us free…' According to John, this is the crux of God's argument: that He wishes to achieve our bliss through our denial of ourselves. The loss of self gives God the opportunity to join with us in a state of bliss.

One of Ruusbroec's most important contributions to mystical thought is his concept of modes. Without modes, he says, no one can live. Modes are delineations and distinctions, categories of action and thought. Weights and measures are also modes. Reason is a mode. So too is sobriety. Discretion as well. However, too much engagement with what John calls 'multiplicity of heart' leads to an inability to invoke its contrary, none other than a state of modelessness. People become too busy about their needs, too entrenched in their modes, believing these to be sufficient to the cultivation of their inner life. Relying too much on their external senses makes it impossible to find inner satisfaction. Provident discretion is good, he says, whereas engaging in too many cares or modes for their own sake is unwise. Moreover, being 'full of images' of alien things, prevents contemplation or being in a state of modelessness.

For John, contemplation is the true way to knowledge. It is the basis of all his thinking with regard to the mystical life. Why? Because it is a "modeless knowing". In his prefatory poem to the *Beguines,* he makes it possible for us to comprehend the power and beauty of his mystical engagement with God:

> Contemplation is a modeless knowing
> Which always remains above reason.
> It cannot descend into the reason
> And reason cannot reach it above itself.
>
> Enlightened modelessness is a sublime mirror
> In which God lets his eternal light shine.
> Modelessness is without manner,
> In which all work of reason fails.
>
> Modelessness is not God,
> But it is the light in which one sees.
> Those who walk in modelessness, in the divine light,
> See into the void.
>
> Modelessness is above reason, not outside it;
> It sees everything without amazement.
> Amazement is below it:
> Contemplative life is without amazement.
>
> Modelessness sees, but it knows not what:
> It is above all neither this nor that.
> Now I must leave rhyming behind
> If I shall clearly describe contemplation.

Here we find ourselves in the presence of a luminous mind contemplating essences in a state of pure unreason.

When a person achieves such a state of pure modelessness, a state of what John calls 'modeless love,' and has acquired the capacity to be annihilated, only then is he able to melt away in love, and so become deiformed – that is, to be transformed into the image of Christ. By way of comparison, he alludes to a red hot iron manifesting all the properties of the fire. 'As far as it is fire it is iron, and as far as it is iron it is fire. Nonetheless, the iron does not become fire nor the fire iron.' Each maintains the integrity of its own matter and nature. Likewise, John says, the human spirit does not become God; but it is given the form of God. Thus a person becomes deiformed. He understands himself to be uplifted to the level of God. He sees himself as part of God's 'depth', and so uplifted in his own super-essence, which is none other than God's essence.

Once more John tires of seeking out the dilemma that lies at the heart of language when it is deliberately subjected to the impress of mystical fervor. He is utterly unable to resist this unfathomable dialectic, given his love of the verbal construct in language itself. One senses that Ruusbroec is drawn to it as iron is to the fire. Nor can he escape the heady vortex of thought that it implies. He longs to be lost in language, to be smothered in the silkiness of words. They are more real to him than what the world offers. He is framed by the mystical artifice of letters. They are like butterflies, dancing above the meadow of his mind. From them he formulates 'humble lowliness,' 'unmoved blessedness,' 'imageless inactivity,' 'eternal lostness,' and 'imageless nudity' as but a few of his radical new concepts. These become talismans for John of Ruusbroec. He has found a way to break down language into its component parts, and then rebuild these as he would have them appertain to what he calls the 'imageless mind of God.' He wrestles, he fights until he begins to *feel* unity 'without difference or distinction,' even as he resorts to language to express what he means. The mystical life has become a state of 'fruitive love' for him in all its aspects.

John of Ruusbroec was one of the great mystical geniuses of his age, indeed of any age. He wrote more treatises than either Meister Eckhart or Therese of Avila during his long life. One is constantly amazed at his output at a time when paper and time were at a premium. Nor had the printing press been invented. Who did he write for? Certainly not for the general public, which would have found his thought all but incomprehensible. He wrote for the few, his confreres in the monastery and to those whom he knew from elsewhere through his letters.

Here is a man who radiated words. They were a manifestation of his light. In him the mystical life reached its zenith. Through him it became a composed method of spiritual growth for men long used to the oppressive imperialism of theology in their lives. John, along with his friends, John Hinkaert and Francis van Coudenberg, together they served notice on the old monastic system by founding their priory of three at Groenendaal, at least initially. They were in the vanguard of a more private order of devotion, one committed to the individual's response to the divinity of Christ. Grote, Tauler, and Thomas a Kempis were deeply indebted to his writings in their desire to further develop the Modern Devotion movement in Germany and the Netherlands.

The effect of his thought is far-reaching, even down to our own time. Modern Dutch poets such as Leo Jansen and Hans Vandervoorde fashioned their own mystical perception through reference to Ruusbroec's imagery. Henry Michaux, another Belgium writer and surrealist

(1899), was deeply influenced by his compatriot. When he wrote 'I write with transport and for myself,' we could be hearing the voice of Ruusbroec himself. He spoke of the act of writing as an exorcism, deliberately so. Without God, however, writers like Michaux could only resort to the nostalgia for nothingness in their bid to find meaning in their lives. It became harder for these modern writers to invoke the mystical life, except elliptically. The notion of living in Christ had been subverted by secularism and the modern condition. For Michaux, as for other modern writers, such a life became an oddity.

Finally, we must confront John of Ruusbroec's unique use of language if we are to understand his importance to mystical thought. He has made the world of neologism his domain. His mysticism is the result of a leap into the unknown. No writer can match him in this respect, not even Eckhart, for the way the use of neologism managed to help him express the sublimity of his thought. He has provided the inexpressible and the mysterious with a syntax of its own. Christ's memory is well served by him, and we should be grateful. It remains to be seen whether his voice will be heard in our own age, where the reign of facts hold such sway over our lives - much more than his gentle empiricism of the spirit.

An uneventful life, and yet a life lived with inner fervor. We are attracted to John of Ruusbroec precisely because, unlike a mystic such as Angela of Foligno, he did not appear to live an openly conflicted life. The forest around his hermitage offered him its protection, its path towards the mystical life. He found a way to make its natural introversion a part of himself. Pure, one-fold clarity became the preserve of this - as he spoke of himself – utterly ghostly man. What was shadowy in his personality, what he called his lack of modefulness, remains, even today, the essence of what he was as a mystical thinker. He found a way to abandon language, even as he embraced its mindfulness.

All things
are too small
to hold me,
I am so vast

In the Infinite
I reach
for the Uncreated

I have touched it,

it undoes me wider than wide

Everything else is too narrow

You know this well,
you who are also there
Hadewijch (13th Cent.)[1]

This is the man who penned *The Sparkling Stone* and *The Book of Supreme Truth.* Both books are late-medieval spiritual classics that reflect a startling grasp of the apophatic nature of philosophic expression which had crept into Christian theology after the translation of Dionysius the Areopagites' *Divine Names* and *Celestial Hierarchies* by John Scotus Erigena in the tenth-century. Ruusbroec's work represents a development of mystical concepts appropriate to an age that had already fully absorbed Neoplatonism and the works of Aristotle. Contemplation, the monastic ideal, and a greater understanding of the ethical requirement of an age much afflicted by disease and political disruption meant that Ruusbroec's vision was of special relevance. He had fashioned a language, an apophatic language, in order to bear the weight of a new dispensation that was about to

English version by Jane Hirshfield

burst upon the world. The humanists of the Renaissance, particularly in Italy, owe much to this man's pioneering work. They were free now to put aside mystical exegesis in their pursuit of the life-loving gifts of classical Greek philosophy. Because of his deep spiritual insights, men like Marsilio Ficino and Francesco Guiciardini could embrace Plato and Aristotle in a new and refreshing way.

Ruusbroec represents the beginning of a modern subjectivity with regard to the inner life. Though he was deeply conventional in his dogmatic understanding of the tenets of Christianity, he nonetheless found a way to circumvent these by resorting to a mystical language that released Christian dogma from its age-old constraints as a repository of piety and ethics. His Christianity, aligned to metaphor and poetry as it was, heralded a revival of mysticism as a spiritual practice that all men could partake of. Now a believer could find solace in his own thoughts rather than simply rely on clerical advice or admonition. The seeds of humanism had been planted, and John of Ruusbroec tended them with love and forbearance throughout his life. In his hands the 'sparkling stone' of the mystical way had been fashioned into a rare and precious gem. We must be thankful for his quiet and retiring genius in enabling this to happen.

James Cowan

2018

THE SPARKLING STONE

PROLOGUE

The man who would live in the most perfect state of Holy Church must be a good and zealous man; an inward and ghostly man; an uplifted and God-seeing man; and an outflowing man to all in common.

Whenever these four things are together in a man, then his state is perfect; and through the increase of grace he shall continually grow and progress in all virtues, and in the knowledge of truth, before God and before all men.

CHAPTER I

THROUGH THREE THINGS A MAN BECOMES GOOD

Hear now three things which constitute a good man. The first, which a good man must have, is a clean conscience without reproach of mortal sin.

And therefore whosoever wishes to become a good man must examine and prove himself with due discernment, from that time onward when he could first have committed sin. And from all these sins he must purge himself, according to the precept and the custom of Holy Church.

The second thing which pertains to a good man is that he must in all things be obedient to God, and to Holy Church, and to his own proper convictions.

And to each of these three he must be equally obedient: so shall he live without care and doubt, and shall ever abide without inward reproach in all his deeds.

The third thing which behoves every good man is that in all his deeds he should have in mind, above all else, the glory of God. And if it happens that by reason of his business or the multiplicity of his works, he has not always God before his eyes, yet at least there should be established in him the intention and desire to live according to the dearest will of God.

Behold, these three things, when they are possessed in this way, make a man good. And whosoever lacks any one of these three is neither good nor in the grace of God; but whenever a man resolves in his heart to fulfil these three points, how wicked soever he may have been before, in that very instant he becomes good, and is susceptible of God, and filled with the grace of God.

CHAPTER II

THROUGH THREE THINGS A MAN BECOMES INWARD

If, further, this good man would become an inward and ghostly man, he needs must have three further things. The first is a heart unencumbered with images; the second is spiritual freedom in his desires, the third is the feeling of inward union with God.

Now let everyone who thinks himself to be ghostly observe himself. He who would have a heart void of images may not possess anything with affection, nor may he cling to any one, or have intercourse with him with attachment of the will; for all intercourse and all affection which do not aim purely at the honour of God bring images into a man's heart, since they are born, not of God, but of the flesh. And so if a man would become spiritual, he must forsake all fleshly lusts and loves and must cleave with longing and love to God alone, and thus possess Him. And through this, all imaginations and all inordinate love towards creatures are cast out. And this loving possession of God makes a man inwardly free from ungodly images; for God is a Spirit, of Whom no one can make to himself a true image. Certainly in this exercise a man should lay hold of good images to help him; such as the Passion of our Lord and all those things that may stir him to greater devotion. But in the possession of God, the man must sink down to that imageless Nudity which is God; and this is the first condition, and the foundation, of a ghostly life.

The second condition is inward freedom. Through this, the man should be able to raise himself towards God in all inward exercises, free from images and encumbrances; that is, in thanksgiving and praise, in worship, in devout prayer and fervent love, and in all those things that may be done by longing and love with the help of the grace of God and through inward zeal in all ghostly exercises.

Through this inward exercise, he reaches the third state; which is that he feels a ghostly union with God. Whosoever then has, in his inward exercise, an imageless and free ascent unto his God, and means nought else but the glory of God, must taste of the goodness of God; and he must feel from within a true union with God. And in this union, the inward and spiritual life is made perfect; for in this union, the desirous power is perpetually enticed anew and stirred to new inward activity. And by each act, the spirit rises upwards to a new union. And so activity and union perpetually renew themselves; and this perpetual renewal in activity and in union is a ghostly life. And so you are now able to see how a man becomes good through the moral virtues and an upright intention; and how he may become ghostly through the inward virtues and union with God. But without these said points, he can neither be good nor ghostly.

CHAPTER III

THROUGH THREE THINGS A MAN BECOMES GOD-SEEING

Further, you must know that if this ghostly man would now become a God-seeing man, he needs must have three other things. The first is the feeling that the foundation of his being is abysmal, and he should possess it in this manner; the second is that his inward exercise should be wayless; the third is that his indwelling should be a divine fruition.

Now understand, you who would live in the spirit, for I am speaking to no one else. The union with God which a spiritual man feels, when the union is revealed to the spirit as being abysmal — that is, measureless depth, measureless height, measureless length and measureless breadth — in this manifestation the spirit perceives that through love it has plunged itself into the depth and has ascended into the height and escaped into the length; and it feels itself to be wandering in the breadth, and to dwell in a knowledge which is ignorance. And through this intimate feeling of union, it feels itself to be melting into the Unity; and, through dying to all things, into the life of God. And there it feels itself to be one life with God. And this is the foundation, and the first point, of the God-seeing life.

And from this there arises the second point, which is an exercise above reason and without condition: for the Divine Unity, of which every God-seeing spirit has entered into possession in love, eternally draws and invites the Divine Persons and all loving spirits into its self. And this inward drawing is felt by each lover, more or less, according to the measure of his love and the manner of his exercise. And whosoever yields himself to this indrawing, and keeps himself therein, cannot fall into mortal sin. But the God-seeing man who has forsaken self and all things, and does not feel himself drawn away because he no longer possesses anything as his own, but stands empty of all, he can always enter, naked and unencumbered with images, into the inmost part of his spirit. There he finds revealed an Eternal Light, and in this light, he feels the eternal demand of the Divine Unity; and he feels himself to be an eternal fire of love, which craves above all else to be one with God. The more he yields to this indrawing or demand, the more he feels it. And the more he feels it, the more he craves to be one with God; for it urges him to pay the debt which is demanded of him by God.

This eternal demand of the Divine Unity kindles within the spirit an eternal fire of love; and though the spirit incessantly pays the debt, an eternal burning continues within it. For, in the transformation within the Unity, all spirits fail in their own activity, and feel nothing else but a burning up of themselves in the simple Unity of God. This simple Unity of God none can feel or possess save he who maintains himself in the immeasurable radiance, and in the love which is above reason and wayless.

In this transcendent state the spirit feels in itself the eternal fire of love; and in this fire of love it finds neither beginning nor end, and it feels itself one with this fire of love. The spirit for ever continues to burn in itself, for its love is eternal; and it feels itself ever more and more to be burnt up in love, for it is drawn and transformed into the Unity of God, where the spirit burns in love. If it observes itself, it finds a distinction and an otherness between itself and God; but where it is burnt up it is undifferentiated and without distinction, and therefore it feels nothing but unity; for the flame of the Love of God consumes and devours all that it can enfold in its Self.

And thus you may see that the indrawing Unity of God is nought else than the fathomless Love, which lovingly draws inward, in eternal fruition, the Father and the Son and all that lives in Them. And in this Love we shall burn and be burnt up without end, throughout eternity; for herein lies the blessedness of all spirits. And therefore we must all found our lives upon a fathomless abyss; that we may eternally plunge into Love, and sink down in the fathomless Depth. And with that same Love, we shall ascend, and transcend ourselves, in the incomprehensible Height. And in that Love which is wayless, we shall wander and stray, and it shall lead us and lose us in the immeasurable Breadth of the Love of God.

And herein we shall flee forth and flee out of ourselves, into the unknown raptures of the Goodness and Riches of God. And therein we shall melt and be melted away, and shall eternally wander and sojourn within the Glory of God. Behold ! by each of these images, I show forth to God-seeing men their being and their exercise, but none else can understand them. For the contemplative life cannot be taught. But where the

Eternal Truth reveals Itself within the spirit all that is needful is taught and learnt.

CHAPTER IV

OF THE SPARKLING STONE, AND OF THE NEW NAME WRITTEN IN THE BOOK OF THE SECRETS OF GOD

And therefore the Spirit of our Lord speaks thus in the Book of the Secrets of God, which St John wrote down: to him that overcometh, He says, that is, to him who overcometh and conquereth himself and all else, will I give to eat of the hidden manna, that is, an inward and hidden savour and celestial joy; and will give him a SPARKLING STONE, and in the stone a new name written which no man knoweth saving HE that receiveth it. This Stone is called a pebble, for it is so small that it does not hurt when one treads on it. This stone is shining white and red like a flame of fire; and it is small and round, and smooth all over, and very light.

By this sparkling stone we mean our Lord Christ Jesus, for He is, according to His Godhead, a shining forth of the Eternal Light, and an irradiation of the glory of God, and a flawless mirror in which all things live. Now to him who overcomes and transcends all things, this sparkling stone is given; and with it he receives light and truth and life. This stone is also like to a fiery flame, for the fiery love of the Eternal Word has filled the whole world with love and wills that all loving spirits be burned up to nothingness in love.

This stone is also so small that a man hardly feels it, even though he treads it underfoot. And that is why it is called calculus, that is, "treadling." And this is made clear to us by St Paul, where he says that the Son of God emptied Himself, and humbled Himself, and took upon Him the form of a servant, and became obedient unto death, even the death of the cross.

And He Himself spoke through the mouth of the Prophet, saying: I am a worm, and no man: a reproach of men and Despised of the people. And He made Himself so small in time that the Jews trod Him under their feet. But they felt Him not; for, had they recognized the Son of God, they had not dared to crucify Him. He is still little and despised in all men's hearts that do not love Him well. This noble stone of which I speak is wholly round and smooth and even all over. That the stone is round teaches us that the Divine Truth has neither beginning nor end; that it is smooth and even all over teaches us that the Divine Truth shall weigh all things evenly, and shall give to each according to his merits; and that which he gives shall be with each throughout eternity.

The last property of this stone of which I will speak is, that it is particularly light; for the Eternal Word of the Father has no weight, nevertheless It bears heaven and earth by Its strength. And It is equally near to all things; yet none can attain It, for It is set on high and goes before all creatures, and reveals Itself where It wills and when It wills; and, in Its lightness, our heavy human nature has climbed above all the heavens, and sits crowned at the right hand of the Father.

Behold, this is the sparkling stone which is given

to the God-seeing man, and in this stone a new name is written, which no man knoweth saving he that receiveth it.

You should know that all spirits in their return towards God receive names; each one in particular, according to the nobleness of its service and the loftiness of its love. For only the first name of innocence, which we receive at baptism, is adorned with the merits of our Lord Jesus Christ. And when we have lost this name of innocence through sin, if we are willing still to follow God — especially in three works which He wishes to work in us — we are baptized once more in the Holy Ghost. And thereby we receive a new name which shall remain with us throughout eternity.

CHAPTER V

OF THE WORKS WHICH GOD WORKS IN ALL IN COMMON AND OF FIVE KINDS OF SINNERS

Hear now what those three works are, which our Lord works in all men if they will submit themselves thereto. The first work which God works in all men in common consists in His calling and inviting them all, without exception, to union with Himself. And as long as a sinner does not follow this call, he must lack all the other gifts which would follow thereafter. Now I have observed that all sinners may be divided into five kinds. To the first kind belong all those who are careless of good works, who through bodily ease and the lust of the senses prefer to live in worldly employments and in multiplicity of heart. All such are unfit to receive the grace of God, and even if they had received it, they would not be able to keep it.

To the second kind belong those who have willingly and wittingly fallen into mortal sin, yet also do good works, and dwell in the fear and awe of the Lord, and love the just, and desire their prayers, and put their trust therein. So long, however, as turning from God and love of sin vanquish and repulse love of God and turning to God, so long these remain unworthy of the grace of God.

The third kind of sinners consists in all unbelievers, and those who err in faith. What good works soever they do, or what lives soever they lead, without the true faith they cannot please God; for true faith is the foundation of all holiness and all virtues.

To the fourth kind belong those who abide in mortal sin without fear and without shame, who care not for God and His gifts, and neglect all virtues. They hold all ghostly life to be hypocrisy and deceit; and they hardly listen to all that one may say to them of God or of the virtues, for they have established themselves as though there were no God, nor heaven, nor hell, and therefore they desire to know of nothing but that which they now perceive and have before them. Behold, all such are rejected and despised by God, for they sin against the Holy Ghost. Yet they may be converted; but this happens with difficulty and seldom.

The fifth kind of sinners are those hypocrites who do outward good works, not for the glory of God and their own salvation, but to acquire a name for holiness, or for the sake of some fleeting thing. Though they may appear holy and good from without, within they are false and turned away from God, and they lack the grace of God and every virtue.

See, I have shown to you five kinds of sinners, who have all been inwardly called to union with God. But so long as a sinner remains in the service of sin, so long he remains deaf and blind and unable to taste, or to feel, all the good that God wishes to work in him.

But whenever a sinner enters into himself, and considers himself, if he be displeased by his sinful life, then he draws near to God. But if he would be obedient to the call and the words of God, he must of his own free will resolve to leave sin and to do penance. And so he becomes one aim and one will with God, and receives the grace of God.

And therefore we should all conceive of God in this way: First of all that, of His free goodness, He calls and invites all men, without distinction, to union with Himself; both the good and the wicked, without exception. Secondly, we should thus comprehend the goodness of God; how He through grace flows forth towards all men who are obedient to the call of God.

Thirdly, we should find and understand clearly in ourselves that we can become one life and one spirit with God, when we renounce ourselves in every way, and follow the grace of God to the height whereto it would guide us. For the grace of God works according to order in every man, after the measure and the way in which he is able to receive it. And thereby, through the universal working of the grace of God, every sinner, if he desires it, receives the discernment and strength which are needful, that he may leave sin and turn towards virtue. And, through that hidden co-operation of the grace of God, every good man can overcome all sins, and can resist all temptations, and can fulfil all virtues, and can persevere in the highest perfection, if he be in all things submissive to the grace of God. For all that we are, and all that we have received, from without and from within, these are all the free gifts of God; for which we must thank and praise Him, and with which we must serve Him, if we are to please Him. But there are many gifts of God which are for the good an aid to, and a source of, virtue; but for the wicked an aid to, and an occasion of, sin: such are health, beauty, wisdom, riches, and worldly dignity. These are the lowest and least precious gifts of God, which God gives for the benefit of all, to His friends and to His enemies, to the good and to the wicked. And with these the good serve God and His friends; but the wicked, their own flesh, and the devil, and the world.

CHAPTER VI

OF THE DIFFERENCE BETWEEN THE HIRELINGS AND THE FAITHFUL SERVANTS OF GOD

Now you may mark this: that some men receive the gifts of God as hirelings, but others as faithful servants of God; and these differ one from another in all in- ward works, that is, in love and intention, in feeling, and in every exercise of the inward life.

Now understand this well: all those who love themselves so inordinately that they will not serve God, save for their own profit and because of their own reward, these separate themselves from God, and dwell in bondage and in their own selfhood; for they seek, and aim at, their own, in all that they do. And therefore, with all their prayers and with all their good works, they seek after temporal things, or may be strive after eternal things for their own benefit and for their own profit. These men are bent upon themselves in an inordinate way; and that is why they ever abide alone with themselves, for they lack the true love which would unite them with God and with all His beloved.

And although these men seem to keep within the law and the commandments of God and of Holy Church, they do not keep within the law of love; for all that they do, they do, not out of love, but from sheer necessity, lest they shall be damned. And, because they are inwardly unfaithful, they dare not trust in God; but their whole inward life is doubt and fear, travail and misery. For they see on the right hand eternal life, and this they are afraid of losing; and they see on the left hand the eternal pains of hell, and these they are afraid of gaining. But all their prayers, all their labour and all the good works, whatsoever they do, to cast out this fear, help them not; for the more inordinately they love themselves, the more they fear hell. And from this you may learn that their fear of hell springs from self-love, which seeks its own.

Now the Prophet, and also the Preacher, say: The fear of the Lord is the beginning of Wisdom. But by this is meant that fear which is exercised upon the right side, where one considers the loss of eternal blessedness; for this fear arises from the natural tendency which every man has in himself to be blessed, that is, to see God. And therefore, even though a man may be faithless to God, yet whenever he truly observes himself from within, he feels himself to be leaning out from himself towards that blessedness which is God. And this blessedness he fears to lose; for he loves himself better than God, and he loves blessedness wholly for his own sake. And therefore he dare not trust in God. And yet this is that Fear of the Lord which is the beginning of wisdom, and is a law to the unfaithful servants of God: for it compels a man to leave sin, and to strive after virtue, and to do good deeds, and these things prepare a man from without to receive the grace of God and become a faithful servant.

But from that very hour in which, with God's help, he can overcome his selfhood — that is to say, when he is so detached from himself that he is able to leave in the keeping of God everything of which he has need — behold, through doing this he is so well pleasing to God that God bestows upon him His grace. And, through grace, he feels true love: and love casts out doubt and fear, and fills the man with hope and trust, and thus he becomes a faithful servant, and means and loves God in all that he does. Behold, this is the difference between the faithful servant and the hireling.

CHAPTER VII

OF THE DIFFERENCE BETWEEN THE FAITHFUL SERVANTS AND THE SECRET FRIENDS OF GOD

We must now observe the great difference which there is between the faithful servants and the inward friends of God. For through grace and the help of God, the faithful servants have chosen to keep the commandments of God, that is, to be obedient to God and Holy Church in all virtues and goodly behaviour: and this is called the outward or active life. But the inward friends of God choose to follow, besides the commandments, the quickening counsels of God; and this is a loving and inward cleaving to God for the sake of His eternal glory, with a willing abandonment of all that one may possess outside God with lust and love. All such friends God calls and invites inwards, and He teaches them the distinctions of inward exercises and many a hidden way of ghostly life. But He sends His servants outwards, that they may be faithful to Him and to His House in every service and in every kind of outward good works.

Behold, thus God gives His grace and His help to each man according to his fitness; that is, according to the way in which he is in tune with God, whether in outward good works or in the inward practice of love. But none can do and feel the inward exercises unless he be wholly turned inward to God. For as long as a man is divided of heart, so long he looks outwards, and is unstable of mind, and is easily swayed by joy and grief in temporal things, for these are still alive within him. And though he may live according to the commandments of God, inwardly he abides in darkness, and knows not what inward exercises may be, nor how these should be practised. But, since he knows and feels that he has God in mind, and in all his works desires to fulfil His dearest will, with this he may be content; for then he knows himself to be free from hypocrisy in his intention, and faithful in his service. And by these two things he contents himself; and it seems to him that outward good works done with a pure intention are more holy and more profitable than any inward exercise whatever, for by the help of God, he has chosen an outward active way of virtue.

And therefore he had rather exercise himself in the diversity of outward works than serve with inward love that same One for Whom he works. And that is the cause why his mind is more filled with the works which he does, than with God, for Whom he does them. And through this tendency to images in his works, he remains an outward man, and is not able to follow the counsels of God; for his exercise is more outward than inward, more of the senses than of the spirit.

Though he is indeed a faithful servant of God in outward works, yet that which the secret friends of God experience remains hidden from, and unknown to him. And this is why certain gross and outward men always condemn and blame the inward and contemplative men, because they have in mind that these are idle. And this was also the reason why Martha complained to our Lord of her sister Mary, because she did not help her in serving; for she believed that she was doing much service and much usefulness, and that her sister was sitting idle and doing nothing. But our Lord gave His judgment and decided between them: He did not blame Martha for her diligence, for her service was good and useful; but He blamed her for her care, and because she was troubled and cast down by a multitude of outward things. And He praised Mary for her inward exercise, and said that One Thing was needful, and that she had chosen the better part, which should not be taken away from her.

That One Thing which is needful for all men is Divine love. The better part is an inward life, with loving adherence to God. This Mary Magdalen had chosen, and this is chosen by the secret friends of God. But Martha chose an outward, unenclosed, and active life; and that is the other part, in which one may serve God, but which is neither so perfect nor so good. And this part is chosen out of love by the faithful servants of God.

But there are found some foolish men who would be so inward that they would neither act nor serve, even in those things of which their neighbour has need. Behold, these are neither secret friends nor faithful servants of God; but they are altogether false and deceived. For no man can follow the counsels of God who will not keep His commandments.

And therefore all secret friends of God are also at the same time faithful servants, wherever this is needful; but all the faithful servants are not secret friends, for the exercise which belongs thereto is unknown to them.

This is the difference between the faithful servants and the secret friends of God.

CHAPTER VIII

OF THE DIFFERENCE BETWEEN THE SECRET FRIENDS AND THE HIDDEN SONS OF GOD

But further we find a more subtle and inward difference, between the secret friends and the hidden sons of God; and yet both these alike by their inward exercise maintain themselves in the Presence of God. But the friends possess their inwardness as an attribute, for they choose the loving adherence to God as best and highest of all that they ever can and will reach: and that is why they cannot with themselves and their own activity penetrate to the imageless Nudity.

For they have, as images and intermediaries between God and themselves, their own being and their own activity. And though in their loving adherence they feel united with God, yet, in this union, they always feel a difference and an otherness between God and themselves. For the simple passing into the Bare and Wayless, they do not know and love: and therefore their highest inward life ever remains in Reason and in Ways. And though they have clear understanding and discernment of all virtues that may be conceived, the simple staring with open heart into the Divine Brightness remains unknown of them. And though they feel themselves uplifted to God in a mighty fire of love, yet they keep something of their own selfhood, and are not consumed and burnt to nothingness in the unity of love.

And though they may desire to live for ever more in the service of God and to please Him eternally, they will not die in God to all the selfhood of their spirit, and receive from Him a God-formed life. And even though they esteem little and count as nothing all consolation and all rest which may come from without, yet they greatly value the gifts of God, and also their own inward works, and the solace and sweetness which they feel within; and thus they rest upon the way, and do not so wholly die to themselves, as to be able to attain the highest beatitude in bare and wayless love. And even if they could practise and apprehend with clear discernment the perfection of loving adherence to God, and all the inward and upward going ways by which one may pass into the Presence of God; yet the wayless passing, and the glorious wandering, in the Superessential Love, wherein neither end, nor beginning, nor way, nor manner, can ever be found, would remain hidden from, and unknown of them.

And so there is a great difference between the secret friends and the hidden sons of God. For the friends feel nought else but a loving and living ascent to God in some wise; but, above this, the sons experience a simple and death-like passing which is in no wise.

The inward life of the friends of our Lord is an upward-striving exercise of love, wherein they desire to remain for ever with their own selfhood; but how one possesses God through bare love above every exercise, in freedom from one's self, this they do not feel. Hence they are always striving upwards towards

God in true faith, and await God and eternal blessedness with sincere hope, and are fastened and anchored to God through perfect charity. And therefore good things have befallen them, for they please God, and God is complaisant unto them: yet for all this, they are not assured of eternal life, for they have not entirely died to themselves and to all selfhood. But all those who abide and endure in their exercise and in that turning to God which they have chosen above all else, these God has chosen in eternity, and their names together with their works are written from eternity in the living book of the Providence of God.

But those who choose other things, and turn their inward faces away from God toward sin, and endure therein (even though their names were written and known of God because of the temporal righteousness which they had practised before), their names shall be blotted out and erased from the Book of Life because they did not persevere unto death, and they shall never more be able to taste of God, nor of any fruit which springs from virtue. And therefore we must needs observe ourselves with diligence, and adorn our turning towards God, from within with inward love, and from without with good works: thus we can await in hope and joy the judgment of God and the coming of our Lord Jesus Christ. But could we renounce ourselves, and all selfhood in our works, we should, with our bare and imageless spirit, transcend all things: and, without intermediary, should be led of the Spirit of God into the Nudity. And then we should feel the certainty that we are indeed the sons of God: for as many as are led by the spirit of God, they are the sons of God, says the Apostle St. Paul.

Nevertheless, you should know that all good and faithful men are the sons of God; for they are all born of the Spirit of God, and the Spirit of God lives in them. And He moves and stirs them — each according to his own capacity — to virtues and good works, wherein they are well pleasing to God. But because of the inequality of their adherence and their exercises, I call some the faithful servants of God, and others to call His secret friends, and others again His hidden sons: nevertheless, they are all servants, friends, and sons, for they all serve and love and mean one God, and they live and work only by the free Spirit of God. And God permits and allows that His friends do and leave undone all those things which are not contrary to His commandments; and for those who are bound by the counsels of God, then this bond also is a commandment. And so no one is disobedient or contrary to God save he who does not keep His commandments; but all those things which God commands and forbids in Scripture, or by Holy Church, or in our conscience, all these things we must do and leave undone, or else be disobedient to God, and lose His grace.

But if we fall into venial sins, this is suffered both by God and by our reason, for we cannot wholly guard against them. And therefore such failings do not make us disobedient, for they do not drive out the grace of God nor our inward peace: nevertheless, we should always lament such lapses, how small soever they may be, and guard against them with all our might.

And by these words I have explained to you what

I said at the beginning: namely, that every man must needs be obedient in all things to God and to Holy Church and to his own conscience; for I do not wish that any should be unjustly offended by my words. And herewith I leave it even as I have said it.

CHAPTER IX

HOW WE MAY BECOME HIDDEN SONS OF GOD, AND ATTAIN TO THE GOD-SEEING LIFE

But I still longed to know how we may become hidden sons of God, and may attain to the God-seeing life. And as to this I have apprehended the following. As it has been said before, we must always live and be watchful in all virtues, and beyond all virtues must forsake this life and die in God; for we must die to sin and be born of God into a life of virtue, and we must renounce ourselves and die in God into an eternal life. And as to this ensues the following instruction:

If we are born of the Spirit of God, we are the sons of grace; and so our whole life is adorned with virtues.

Thereby we overcome all that is contrary to God; for St John says, Whatsoever is born of God overcometh the world. In this birth all good men are sons of God. And the Spirit of God kindles and stirs each one of them in particular to those virtues and to those good works for which he is in readiness, and of which he is capable. And so they please God all in common, and each in particular, according to the measure of his love and the nobleness of his exercise; nevertheless, they do not feel established nor possessed of God, nor assured of eternal life, for they may still turn away and fall into sin. And that is why I call them rather servants and friends, than sons. But when we transcend ourselves, and become, in our ascent towards God, so simple that the naked love in the height can lay hold of us, where love enfolds love, above every exercise of virtue — that is, in our Origin, of Which we are spiritually born — then we cease, and we and all our selfhood die in God. And in this death we become hidden sons of God, and find a new life within us: and that is eternal life. And of these sons, St Paul says: You are dead, and

YOUR LIFE IS HID WITH CHRIST IN GOD

Now understand, the explanation of this is as follows. In our approach to God, we must carry with us ourselves and all our works, as a perpetual sacrifice to God; and in the Presence of God, we must forsake ourselves and all our works, and, dying in love, go forth from all creatureliness into the superessential richness of God: there we shall possess God in an eternal death to ourselves. And that is why the Spirit of God says in the book of the Divine Secrets: Blessed are the dead which die in the Lord.

Justly He calls them the blessed dead, for they remain eternally dead and lost to themselves in the fruitive Unity of God. And they die in love ever anew, through the indrawing transformation of that same Unity. Further, the Spirit of God says: They may rest from their labours, and their works do follow them. In the ordinary state of grace, when we are born of God into a ghostly and virtuous life, we carry our works before us, as an offering to God; but in the wayless state, where we die back into God in an eternal and blessed life, there our good works follow us, for they are one life with us.

When we go towards God by means of the virtues, God dwells in us; but when we go out from ourselves and from all else, then we dwell in God. So soon as we have faith, hope and charity, we have received God, and He dwells in us with His grace, and He sends us out as His faithful servants, to keep His commandments. And He calls us in again as His secret friends, so soon as we are willing to follow His counsels; and He names us openly as His sons so soon as we live in opposition to the world. But if above all things we would taste God, and feel eternal life in ourselves, we must go forth into God with our feeling, above reason; and there we must abide, onefold, empty of ourselves, and free from images, lifted up by love into the simple bareness of our intelligence. For when we go out in love beyond and above all things, and die to all observation in ignorance and in darkness, then we are wrought and transformed through the Eternal Word, Who is the Image of the Father.

In this idleness of our spirit, we receive the Incomprehensible Light, which enwraps us and penetrates us, as the air is penetrated by the light of the sun. And this Light is nothing else than a fathomless staring and seeing. What we are, that we behold; and what we behold, that we are: for our thought, our life, and our being are uplifted in simplicity, and made one with the Truth which is God. And therefore in this simple staring we are one life and one spirit with God: and this I call a contemplative life. As soon as we cleave to God through love, we practise the better part; but when we gaze thus into our superessence, we possess God utterly. With this contemplation, there is bound up an exercise which is wayless, that is to say, a nought - ing of life; for, where we go forth out of ourselves into darkness and the abysmal Waylessness, there shines perpetually the simple ray of the Splendour of God, in which we are grounded, and which draws us out of ourselves into the superessence, and into the immersion of love.

And with this sinking into love there is always bound up a practice of love which is wayless; for love cannot be lazy, but would search through and through and taste through and through the fathomless richness which lives in the ground of her being, and this is a hunger which cannot be appeased. But a perpetual striving after the un-attainable — this is swimming against the stream.

One can neither leave it nor grasp it, neither do with-out it nor attain it, neither be silent on it nor speak of it, for it is above reason and understanding, and it transcends all creatures; and therefore we can never reach nor overtake it. But we should abide within ourselves: there we feel that the Spirit of God is driving us and enkindling us in this restlessness of love. And we should abide above ourselves. And then we feel that the Spirit of God is drawing us out of ourselves and burning us to nothingness in His Selfhood; that is, in the Superessential Love with which we are one, and which we possess more deeply and more widely than all else.

This possession is a simple and abysmal tasting of all good and of eternal life; and in this tasting we are swallowed up above reason and without reason, in the deep Quiet of the Godhead, which is never moved. That this is true we can only know by our own feeling, and in no other way. For how this is, or where, or what, neither reason nor practice can come to know: and therefore our ensuing exercise always remains wayless, that is, without manner. For that abysmal Good which we taste and possess, we can neither grasp nor understand; neither can we enter into it by ourselves or by means of our exercises. And so we are poor in ourselves, but rich in God; hungry and thirsty in ourselves, drunken and fulfilled in God; busy in ourselves, idle in God. And thus we shall remain throughout eternity. But without the exercise of love, we can never possess God; and whosoever thinks or feels otherwise is deceived. And thus we live wholly in God, where we possess our blessedness; and we live wholly in ourselves, where we exercise ourselves in love towards God. And though we live wholly in God and wholly in ourselves, yet it is but one life; but it is twofold and opposite according to our feeling, for poor and rich, hungry and satisfied, busy and idle, these things are wholly contrary to one another.

Yet with this our highest honour is bound up, now and in eternity: for we cannot wholly become God and lose our created being, this is impossible. Did we, however, remain wholly in ourselves, sundered from God, we should be miserable and unblest. And therefore we should feel ourselves living wholly in God and wholly in ourselves; and between these two feelings we should find nothing else but the grace of God and the exercise of our love. For out of our highest feeling, the brightness of God shines into us, which teaches us truth, and moves us towards every virtue and in eternal love towards God. If we follow this brightness without pause, back into that Source from whence it comes forth, there we feel nothing but a quenching of our spirit and an irretrievable down-sinking into simple and fathomless love.

Could we continue to dwell there with our simple gaze, we should always so feel it; for our immersion and transformation in God continues without ceasing in eternity, if we have gone forth from ourselves, and God is ours in the immersion of love. For if we possess God in the immersion of love — that is, if we are lost to ourselves — God is our own and we are His own: and we sink ourselves eternally and irretrievably in our own possession, which is God.

This immersion is essential, and is closely bound up with the state of love: and so it continues whether we sleep or whether we wake, whether we know it or whether we know it not. And so it does not earn for us any new degree of reward; but it maintains us in the possession of God and of all that good which we have received. And this down-sinking is like a river, which without pause or turning back ever pours into the sea; since this is its proper resting-place. So likewise when we possess God alone, the down-sinking of our being, with the love that belongs to it, flows forth, without return, into a fathomless experience which we possess, and which is our proper resting-place. Were we always simple, and could we always contemplate with the same recollection, we should always have the same experience.

Now this immersion is above all virtues, and above every exercise of love; for it is nothing else than an eternal going out from ourselves, with a clear looking forward, into an otherness or difference towards which, outside ourselves, we tend as towards our blessedness. For we feel an eternal yearning toward something other than what we are ourselves. And this is the most inward and hidden distinction which we can feel between God and ourselves, and beyond it there is no difference any more. But our reason abides here with open eyes in the darkness, that is, in an abysmal ignorance; and in this darkness, the abysmal splendour remains covered and hidden from us, for its overwhelming unfathomableness blinds our reason. But it enwraps us in simplicity, and transforms us through its selfhood: and thus we are brought forth by God, out of our selfhood, into the immersion of love, in which we possess blessedness, and are one with God.

When we are thus made one with God, there abides within us a quickening knowledge and an active love; for without our own knowledge, we cannot possess God; and without the practice of love, we cannot be united with God, nor remain one with Him. For if we could be blessed without our knowledge, then a stone, which has no knowledge, could also be blessed.

Were I lord over all the world and knew it not, how would it profit me? And therefore we shall ever know and feel that we taste and possess; and this is testified by Christ Himself, where He speaks thus of us to His Father: This, He says, is life eternal, that they should know thee, the only true God, and Jesus Christ,

Whom Thou hast sent. And by this you may understand that our eternal life consists in knowledge with discernment.

CHAPTER X

HOW WE, THOUGH ONE WITH GOD, MUST ETERNALLY REMAIN OTHER THAN GOD

Though I have said before that we are one with God, and this is taught us by Holy Writ, yet now I will say that we must eternally remain other than God, and distinct from Him, and this too is taught us by Holy Writ. And we must understand and feel both within us, if all is to be right with us.

And therefore I say further: that from the Face of God, or from our highest feeling, a brightness shines upon the face of our inward being, which teaches us the truth of love and of all virtues: and especially are we taught in this brightness to feel God and ourselves in four ways. First, we feel God in His grace; and when we apprehend this, we cannot remain idle. For like as the sun, by its splendour and its heat, enlightens and gladdens and makes fruitful the whole world, so God does to us through His grace: He enlightens and gladdens and makes fruitful all men who desire to obey Him. If, however, we would feel God within us, and have the fire of His love ever more burning within us, we must, of our own free will, help to kindle it in four ways: We must abide within ourselves, united with the fire through inwardness. And we must go forth from ourselves towards all good men with loyalty and brotherly love. And we must go beneath ourselves in penance, betaking ourselves to all good works, and resisting our inordinate lusts. And we must ascend above ourselves with the flame of this fire, through devotion, and thanksgiving, and praise, and fervent prayer, and must ever cleave to God with an upright intention and with sensible love.

And thereby God continues to dwell in us with His grace; for in these four ways is comprehended every exercise which we can do with the reason, and in some wise, but without this exercise no one can please God. And he who is most perfect in this exercise, is nearest to God. And therefore it is needful for all men; and above it none can rise save the contemplative men. And thus, in this first way, we feel God within us through His grace, if we wish to belong to Him.

Secondly: when we possess the God-seeing life, we feel ourselves to be living in God; and from out of that life in which we feel God in ourselves, there shines forth upon the face of our inward being a brightness which enlightens our reason, and is an intermediary between ourselves and God. And if we with our enlightened reason abide within ourselves in this brightness, we feel that our created life incessantly immerses itself in its eternal life. But when we follow the brightness above reason with a simple sight, and with a willing leaning out of ourselves, toward our highest life, there we experience the transformation of our whole selves in God; and thereby we feel ourselves to be wholly enwrapped in God.

And, after this, there follows the third way of feeling; namely, that we feel ourselves to be one with God; for, through the transformation in God, we feel ourselves to be swallowed up in the fathomless abyss of our eternal blessedness, wherein we can nevermore find any distinction between ourselves and God. And this is our highest feeling, which we cannot experience in any other way than in the immersion in love. And therefore, so soon as we are uplifted and drawn into our highest feeling, all our powers stand idle in an essential fruition; but our powers do not pass away into nothingness, for then we should lose our created being. And as long as we stand idle, with an inclined spirit, and with open eyes, but without reflection, so long we can contemplate and have fruition.

But, at the very moment in which we seek to prove and to comprehend what it is that we feel, we fall back into reason, and there we find a distinction and an otherness between ourselves and God, and find God outside ourselves in incomprehensibility. And hence the fourth way of distinction; which is, that we feel God and ourselves.

Hereby we now find ourselves standing in the Presence of God; and the truth which we receive from the Face of God teaches us that God would be wholly ours and that He wills us to be wholly His. And in that same moment in which we feel that God would be wholly ours, there arises within us a gaping and eager craving which is so hungry and so deep and so empty that, even though God gave all that He could give, if he gave not Himself, we should not be appeased. For, whilst we feel that He has given Himself and yielded Himself to our untrammeled craving, that we may taste of Him in every way that we can desire — and of this we learn the truth in His sight — yet all that we taste, against all that we lack, is but like to a single drop of water against the whole sea: and this makes our spirit burst forth in fury and in the heat and the restlessnesss of love. For the more we taste, the greater our craving and our hunger; for the one is the cause of the other.

And thus it comes about that we struggle in vain. For we feed upon His Immensity, which we cannot devour, and we yearn after His Infinity, which we cannot attain: and so we cannot enter intoGod nor can God enter into us, for in the untamed fury of love we are not able to renounce ourselves.

And therefore the heat is so unmeasured that the exercise of love between ourselves and God flashes to and fro like the lightning in the sky; and yet we cannot be consumed in its ardour. And in this storm of love our activity is above reason and wayless; for love longs for that which is impossible to it, and reason teaches that love is in the right, but reason can neither counsel love nor dissuade her.

For as long as we inwardly perceive that God would be ours, the goodness of God touches our eager craving: and therefrom springs the wildness of love, for the touch which pours forth from God stirs up this wildness, and demands our activity, that is, that we should love eternal love. But the inward-drawing touch draws us out of ourselves, and calls us to be melted and noughted in the Unity. And in this inward- drawing touch, we feel that God wills us to be His; and therefore, we must renounce ourselves and leave Him to work our blessedness. But where He touches us by the outpouring touch, He leaves us to ourselves, and makes us free, and sets us in His Presence, and teaches us to pray in the spirit and to ask in freedom, and shows us His incomprehensible riches in such manifold ways as we are able to grasp.

For everything that we can conceive, wherein is consolation and joy, this we find in Him without measure. And therefore, when our feeling shows us that He with all these riches would be ours and dwell in us for ever more, then all the powers of the soul open themselves, and especially the desirous power; for all the rivers of the grace of God pour forth, and the more we taste of them, the more we long to taste; and the more we long to taste, the more deeply we press into contact with Him; and the more deeply we press into contact with God, the more the flood of His sweetness flows through us and over us; and the more we are thus drenched and flooded, the better we feel and know that the sweetness of God is incomprehensible and unfathomable.

And therefore the prophet says: O taste, and see that the Lord is sweet. But he does not say how sweet He is, for God's sweetness is without measure; and therefore we can neither grasp it nor swallow it. And this is also testified by the bride of God in the Song of Songs, where she says: I sat down under his Shadow, with great delight, and his fruit was sweet to my taste.

CHAPTER XI

OF THE GREAT DIFFERENCE BETWEEN THE BRIGHTNESS OF THE SAINTS AND THE HIGHEST BRIGHTNESS TO WHICH WE CAN ATTAIN IN THIS LIFE

There is a great difference between the brightness of the saints and the highest brightness or enlightenment to which we may attain in this life. For it is only the shadow of God which enlightens our inward wilderness, but on the high mountains of the Promised Land there is no shadow: and yet it is one and the same Sun, and one radiance, which enlightens both our wilderness and the high mountains. But the state of the saints is transparent and shining, and therefore they receive the brightness without intermediary: but our state is still mortal and gross, and this sets up an obstacle which causes the shadow, which so darkens our understanding that we cannot know God and heavenly things so clearly as the saints can and do. For as long as we dwell in the shadow, we cannot see the sun in itself; but Now we see through A glass darkly, says St Paul. Yet the shadow is so enlightened by the sunshine that we can perceive the distinctions between all the virtues, and all the truth which is profitable to our mortal state.

But if we would become one with the brightness of the Sun, we must follow love, and go out of ourselves into the Wayless, and then the Sun will draw us with our blinded eyes into Its own brightness, in which we shall possess unity with God. So soon we feel and understand ourselves thus, we are in that contemplative life which is within reach of our mortal state.

The state of the Jews, according to the Old Testament, was cold and in the night, and they walked in darkness. And they Dwelt in the land of the shadow of death, says the prophet Isaias. The shadow of death came forth from original sin; and therefore they had all to endure the lack of God. But though our state in the Christian faith is but still in the cool and morning hour; yet for us the day has dawned. And therefore we shall walk in the light, and shall sit down in the shadow, of God; and His grace shall be an intermediary between ourselves and God. And, through it, we shall overcome all things, and shall die to all things, and shall pass without hindrance into the unity of God. But the state of the saints is warm and bright; for they live and walk in the noon- tide, and see with open and enlightened eyes the brightness of the Sun, for the glory of God flows through them and overflows in them. And each one according to the degree of his enlightenment, tastes and knows the fruits of all the virtues which have there been gathered together by all spirits.

But that they taste and know the Trinity in the Unity, and the Unity in the Trinity, and know themselves united therewith, this is the highest and all-surpassing food which makes them drunken, and causes them to rest in Its Selfhood. And This it was that the bride in the Book of Love desired, when she said unto Christ: Tell me, O Thou Whom my soul loveth, where thou feedest, where thou makest Thy flock to rest at noon, that is, in the light of glory, as St Bernard says; for all the food which is given to us here, in the morning hour and in the shadow, is but a foretaste of the food that is to come in the noon-tide of the glory of God.

Yet the bride of our Lord gloried in having sat under the shadow of God, and that His fruit was sweet to her taste. Whenever we feel that God touches us from within, we taste of His fruit and His food: for His touch is His food. And His touch is both in-drawing and outpouring, as I have said before. In His indrawing, we must be wholly His: thereby we learn to die and to behold. But in His outpouring, He wills to be wholly ours: and then He teaches us to live in the riches of the virtues. In His indrawing-touch all our powers forsake us, and then we sit under His shadow, and His fruit is sweet to our taste, for the Fruit of God is the Son of God, Whom the Father brings forth in our spirit.

This Fruit is so infinitely sweet to our taste that we can neither swallow It nor assimilate It, but It rather absorbs us into Itself and assimilates us with Itself. And whenever this Fruit draws us inward and touches us, we abandon, forsake, and overcome all other things. And in this overcoming of all things, we taste of the hidden manna, which shall give us eternal life; for we receive the sparkling stone, of which I have spoken heretofore, in which our new names were written before the beginning of the world.

This is the New name which no man knoweth

but he that receiveth it. And whosoever feels himself to be for ever united with God, he possesses his name according to the measure of his virtues, and of his introversion, and of his union. And, that every one may obtain his name and possess it in eternity, the Lamb of God, that is, the manhood of our Lord, has delivered Itself up to death; and has opened for us the Book of Life, wherein are written all the names of the elect. And these names cannot be blotted out, for they are one with the Living Book, which is the Son of God. And that same death has broken for us the seals of the Book, so that all virtues may be fulfilled according to the eternal Providence of God.

And so, in the measure in which each man can overcome himself, and can die to all things, he feels the touch of the Father drawing him inward; and then he tastes the sweetness of the Inborn Fruit, Which is the Son; and in this tasting the Holy Ghost teaches him that he is the heir of God. But in these three points no one is like to another in every respect. And therefore each one has been named separately, and his name is continually made new through new graces and new works of virtue. And therefore every knee shall bow before the Name of Jesus, for He has fought for our sake, and has conquered. And He has enlightened our darkness, and has fulfilled all the virtues in the highest degree. And so His name is lifted up above all other names, for He is the King and the Prince over all the elect. And in His name we are called and chosen, and adorned with grace and with virtues, and look for the glory of God.

CHAPTER XII

OF THE TRANSFIGURATION OF CHRIST ON MOUNT THABOR

And so, that the Name of Christ may be exalted and glorified in us, we should follow Him up the mountain of our bare intelligence, 1 even as Peter, James, and John followed Him on to mount Thabor. Thabor means in our tongue an increase of light. So soon as we are like Peter in knowledge of truth, and like James in the overcoming of the world, and like John in fulness of grace possessing the virtues in righteousness; then Jesus brings us up on to the mountain of our bare intelligence to a hidden solitude, and reveals Himself to us in glory and in Divine brightness.

And, in His name, His Father in heaven opens to us the living book of His Eternal Wisdom. And the Wisdom of God enfolds our bare vision and the simplicity of our spirit in a wayless, simple fruition of all good without distinction; and here there are indeed seeing and knowing, tasting and feeling, essence and life, having and being: and all this is one in our transcendence in God. And before this transcendence we are all set, each in his own particular way; and our heavenly Father, of His wisdom and goodness, endows each one in particular according to the nobility of his life and his practice. And therefore, if we ever remained with Jesus on mount Thabor, that is, upon the mountain of our bare thought, we should continually experience a growth of new light and new truth;

for we should ever hear the voice of the Father, Who touches us, pouring forth with grace, and drawing us inward into the unity.

The voice of the Father is heard by all who follow our Lord Jesus Christ, for He says of them all: "These are My chosen sons, in whom I am well pleased." And, through this good pleasure, each one receives grace, according to the measure and the way in which God is well-pleasing unto him. And therefrom, between our pleasure in God, and God's pleasure in us, there arises the practice of true love. And so each one tastes of his name and his office and the fruit of his exercise. And here all good men abide, hidden from those who live in the world; for these are dead before God and have no name, and therefore they can neither feel nor taste that which belongs to those who live indeed.

The outpouring touch of God quickens us with life in the spirit, and fulfills us with grace, and enlightens our reason, and teaches us to know truth and to discern the virtues, and keeps us stable in the Presence of God, with such a great strength that we are able to endure all the tasting, all the feeling, and all the outpouring gifts of God without our spirits failing us. But the indra wing-touch of God demands of us, that we should be one with God, and go forth from ourselves, and die into blessedness, that is, into the Eternal Love Which embraces the Father and the Son in one fruition. And therefore when we have climbed with Jesus on to the mountain of our bare thought; and if, then, we follow Him with a single and simple gaze, with inward pleasure, and with fruitive inclination, we feel the fierce heat of the Holy

Ghost, burning and melting us into the Unity of God. For when we are one with the Son, and lovingly return towards our Beginning, then we hear the voice of the Father, touching us and drawing us inward; for He says to all His chosen in His Eternal Word: This is My beloved Son, in Whom I am well pleased.

For you should know that the Father with the Son, and the Son with the Father, have conceived an eternal satisfaction in regard to this: that the Son should take upon Himself our manhood, and die, and bring back all the chosen to their Beginning.

And so soon as we are uplifted through the Son into our Origin, we hear the voice of the Father, which draws us inward, and enlightens us with eternal truth. And truth shows to us the wide-opened good-pleasure of God, in which all good-pleasure begins and ends. There all our powers fail us, and we fall from ourselves into our wide-opened contemplation, and become all One and one All, in the loving embrace of the Threefold Unity. Whenever we feel this union, we are one being and one life and one blessedness with God. And there all things are fulfilled and all things are made new; for when we are baptized into the wide embrace of the Love of God, the joy of each one of us becomes so great and so special that he can neither think of nor care for the joy of anyone else; for then each one is himself a Fruition of Love, and he cannot and dare not seek for anything beyond his own.

CHAPTER XIII

HOW WE OUGHT TO HAVE FRUITION OF GOD

If a man would have fruition of God, three things are needful thereto; these are, true peace, inward silence, and loving adherence.

Whosoever would find true peace between himself and God must love God in such a way that he can, with a free heart, renounce for the glory of God everything which he does or loves inordinately, or which he possesses, or can possess, contrary to the glory of God. This is the first thing which is needful to all men.

The second thing is an inward silence; that is, that a man should be empty and free from images of all things which he ever saw or of which he ever heard.

The third thing is a loving adherence to God, and this adherence is itself fruition; for whosoever cleaves to God out of pure love, and not for his own profit, he enjoys God in truth, and feels that he loves God and that God loves him.

There are still three other points, which are higher still, and which establish a man and make him able to enjoy and to feel God continually, if it be His good will to have it so.

The first of these points is to rest in Him Whom one enjoys; that is, where love is overcome by the lover, and love is taken possession of by the lover, in bare Essential Love. There love has fallen in love with the lover, and each is all to the other, in possession and in rest.

From this there follows the second: and this is called a falling asleep in God; that is, when the spirit immerses itself, and knows not how, nor where, nor in what it is.

And therefrom follows the last point that can be put into words, that is, when the spirit beholds a Darkness into which it cannot enter with the reason. And there it feels itself dead and lost to itself, and one with God without difference and without distinction. And when it feels itself one with God, then God Himself is its peace and its enjoyment and its rest. And this is an unfathomable abyss wherein man must die to himself in blessedness, and must live again in virtues, whenever love and its stirring demand it. Lo! if you feel these six points within you, then you feel all that I have, or could have, said before. And introversion is as easy to you, and contemplation and fruition are as ready to you, as your life according to nature. And from these riches there comes that common life of which I promised to speak to you at the beginning.

CHAPTER XIV

OF THAT COMMON LIFE WHICH COMES FROM THE CONTEMPLATION AND FRUITION OF GOD

The man who is sent down by God from these heights into the world is full of truth and rich in all virtues. And he seeks not his own but the glory of Him Who has sent him. And hence he is just and truthful in all things, and he possesses a rich and a generous ground, which is set in the richness of God: and therefore he must always spend himself on those who have need of him; for the living fount of the Holy Ghost, which is his wealth, can never be spent. And he is a living and willing instrument of God, with which God works whatsoever He wills and howsoever He wills; and these works he reckons not as his own, but gives all the glory to God. And so he remains ready and willing to do in the virtues all that God commands, and strong and courageous in suffering and enduring all that God allows to befall him.

And by this he possesses a universal life, for he is ready alike for contemplation and for action, and is perfect in both of them. And none can have this universal life save the God-seeing man; and none can contemplate and enjoy God save he who has within himself the six points, ordered as I have described heretofore. And therefore, all those are deceived who fancy themselves to be contemplative, and yet inordinately love, practice, or possess, some creaturely thing; or who fancy that they enjoy God before they are empty of images, or that they rest before they enjoy. All such are deceived; for we must make ourselves fit for God with an open heart, with a peaceful conscience, with naked contemplation, without hypocrisy, in sincerity and truth. And then we shall mount up from virtue unto virtue, and shall see God, and shall enjoy Him, and in Him shall become one with Him, in the way which I have shown to you. That this be done in all of us, so help us God. Amen.

THE BOOK OF SUPREME TRUTH

THE BOOK OF SUPREME TRUTH

PROLOGUE

The prophet Samuel mourned for King Saul, though he knew well that God had rejected him and his issue from being kings in Israel: this was because of his pride, and because he did not obey God and the prophet who spoke in His name. We may also read in the Gospel, that the disciples of our Lord pleaded with Him for the Gentile woman of Canaan, to send her away, that is, to do unto her that which she desired; for she cried after Him.

So likewise I might say that we must mourn for all such deceived men as think themselves to be kings in Israel; for they believe themselves to be lifted up above other good men, into a lofty and God-seeing life. And yet they are proud and wittingly and willingly disobedient to God and the law and the Holy Church and every virtue. And like as Saul rent the mantle of the prophet Samuel, they endeavour to rend asunder the unity of the Christian faith, and all true doctrine and virtuous life. Whosoever persist herein, they are separated and shut out from the kingdom of eternal contemplation, even as Saul was shut out from the kingdom of Israel. But that humble little woman of Canaan, though she was Gentile and a stranger, had faith and hope in God, and acknowledged and confessed her littleness before Christ and His apostles: and so she received grace and health and all that she desired. For God exalts the humble, and fills them with grace and all virtues; and He resists the proud, and these remain empty of all good.

CHAPTER I

WHEREFORE THIS BOOK WAS WRITTEN

Certain of my friends have desired and besought me, that I should show and make plain in a few words and according to my best cunning, shortly and clearly, how I understand and feel the truth of all the highest teachings that I have written before; so that none should take offence at my words, but everyone should profit by them. And this I willingly consent to do. I will, with God's help, teach the humble who love virtue and truth; and, with the same words, I shall inwardly vex and darken the false and the proud: for to these my words will be displeasing and contrary, and this the proud cannot endure, but it provokes them to anger.

CHAPTER II

A SHORT REPETITION OF ALL THE HIGHEST TEACHINGS WRITTEN BY THE AUTHOR

Behold, I have said this: that the contemplative lover of God is united with God through means, and also without means, and thirdly, without difference or distinction; and this I find in nature, and in grace, and also in glory. Further I have said that never creature may be or become so holy that it loses its created being and becomes God; even the soul of our Lord Jesus Christ shall ever remain creature, and other than God. Yet, none the less, we must all be lifted up above ourselves into God, and become one spirit with God in love; and then we shall be blessed. And therefore mark my words and my meaning, and understand me aright as to what is the condition and the way to our eternal blessedness.

CHAPTER III

OF THE UNION THROUGH MEANS

And next, I will say that all good men are united with God through means. These means are the grace of God, and the sacraments of Holy Church, and the Divine virtues, faith, hope and charity, and a virtuous life according to the commandments of God; and to these there belongs a death to sin and to the world and to every inordinate lust of nature. And through these, we remain united with Holy Church, that is, with all good men; and with these, we obey God, and are one will with Him, even as an orderly convent is united with its Superior: and without this union none can please God nor be saved. Whosoever keeps this union through these means unto the end of his life, he shall be one of those of whom Christ says unto His Father in heaven in the Gospel of St John: Father, I will that they also whom Thou hast given Me be with Me where I am: that they may behold my glory which thou hast given Me.

And in another place He says that His servants shall sit down to meet — that is, in the richness and the fulness of those virtues which they have exercised — and He will go one to another and will minister unto them of His glory which He has achieved. And He will generously impart and reveal to His beloved, to each one specially and separately — more or less according as he is worthy of it and can lay hold of it — the loftiness of His glory and honour, which He alone has earned by the merits of His life and His death. Thus all saints shall be forever with Christ, each in his own order and in the degree of glory which he has earned through God's help by his works.

And Christ, according to His manhood, shall be set above all saints, and above all angels; as a prince of all glory and all honour; the which pertain to His manhood alone above all creatures.

Behold, thus you may understand how we are united with God through means, both here in grace and hereafter in glory. But there is a great distinction and a great difference in these means, and this is true both as regards life and reward, as I have told you. And this was well understood by St Paul, when he said that he had A desire to depart and to be with Christ. But he did not say that he had a desire to be Christ Himself or God; as is done by some unbelieving and perverse men, who say that they have no God, but that they are so wholly dead to themselves, and united with God, that they have themselves become God.

CHAPTER IV

OF THE MEN WHO PRACTISE A FALSE VACANCY

Behold, such folk, by means of a onefold simplification and a natural tendency, are turned in upon the bareness of their own being; and therefore they think eternal life is and shall be nought else but an enduring state of beatitude, without distinction in order in holiness or in reward. Yea, all such are so deep in error that they say that the Persons shall pass away into the Godhead, and that nought else shall remain in eternity than the essential substance of the Godhead; and that all blessed spirits shall be so simply absorbed with God in the Essential Blessedness that nothing shall remain beside it, neither willing nor working, nor the discerning knowledge of any creature whatsoever.

Behold, these men have gone astray into the vacant and blind simplicity of their own being, and they seek for blessedness in bare nature; for they are so simply and so idly united with the bare essence of their souls, and with that wherein God always is, that they have neither zeal, nor cleaving to God, neither from without, nor from within. For in the highest part into which they have entered, they feel nothing but the simplicity of their own proper being, depending upon the Being of God. And the onefold simplicity which they there possess, they take to be God, because they find a natural rest therein. And so they think themselves to be God in their simple ground; for they lack true faith, hope and charity. And, because of the naked emptiness which they feel and possess, they say that they are without knowledge and without love, and are exempt from the virtues. And so they endeavour to live without heeding their conscience, what wickedness soever they commit.

And they are careless of the sacraments, and of all virtues, and of all the practices of Holy Church, and believe that they have no need of them: for they fancy in their folly that they have passed beyond all these things, but imperfect men, they say, have need of them. And some men have become so accustomed to and deep-rooted in this simplification that they would know and heed as little of all the works which God has wrought, and all that Scripture teaches, as though not one line had ever been written; for they believe themselves to have found and to possess that for the sake of which all Scriptures have been made, namely, the blind essential rest which they feel.

But in fact they have lost God and all the ways which may lead to Him; for they have no more inwardness, nor more devotion, nor holy practices, than a dead beast has. Yet they sometimes approach the sacraments, and at times they quote the Scriptures, that thus they may the better dissimulate and cover themselves; and they like to take some dark saying of Scripture, which they can falsely turn to their own sense, so that they may please other simple men, and may draw them into the false vacancy which they themselves feel, j Behold, these folk think themselves wise and subtle beyond any one else, and yet they are the most coarse and crude of all men living; for that which even Pagans and Jews and bad Christians, learned and unlearned, find and understand through their natural reason, these wretched men neither can nor will attain.

You may cross yourselves against the devil, but beware earnestly of these perverted men, and take care lest you should not recognise them in their words and works. For they would teach, and be taught of none; they would reprove, and be reproved of none; they would command, and obey none. They would oppress others, but no one may oppress them; they wish to say whatever they like, but will endure no contradiction; they recognise only their own self-will and are subject to no one; and this they take to be ghostly freedom.

They practise the liberty of the flesh, for they give to the body whatsoever it lusts after; and this they take to be natural freedom. They have unified themselves in a blind and dark vacancy of their own being; and there, they think, they are one with God, and they. take this for the Eternal Blessedness. And they have entered into this, and have taken possession of it, through self-will and their natural tendency; and therefore they imagine themselves to be set above the law and above the commandments of God and Holy Church. For, above that essential rest which they possess, they feel neither God nor any otherness; for the Divine light has not shone into their dimness. And this is because they have neither sought after it through active love nor through supernatural freedom. And thus they have lost truth and every virtue, and have fallen into a perverted unlikeness; for they make it a part of the highest holiness that a man should yield to all that concerns his nature, and be without restraint, so that he may abide, with an inclined spirit, in vacancy; and that as regards the lusts of the flesh whenever they move him, he should turn outwards, that the flesh being satisfied, he may quickly escape from the image and may return once more unencumbered into the bare vacancy of his spirit.

Lo! this is a fruit of hell, which grows from their unbelief; and therewith shall unbelief be nourished even in death. For, when the time has come and their nature is weighed down with bitter woe and the sorrow of death, then they are filled with images and unrest and inward fear; and they lose their vacant introversion in quietude, and fall into such despair that none can console them, and they die like mad dogs. And their vacancy shall bring them no reward, and those who worked wicked works, and died in them, shall go to the eternal flames, as our faith teaches.

I have shown to you the evil and the good side by side, so that you may so much the better understand the good and be able to guard against the evil. You shall abhor and fly from such folk, for, how holy soever they seem in their conduct, in works, in dress and demeanour, they are the mortal enemies of your soul. For they are the devil's ministers, and the most noxious of all who now live to simple and unlearned men of good-will. But I will leave this subject, and go back again to the matter with which I first began.

CHAPTER V

OF THE UNION WITHOUT MEANS

You may remember that I showed heretofore how all saints and all good men are united with God through means. Now I will further show to you how they are all united with God without means. But in this life there are but few who are meet for this, and sufficiently enlightened to feel and understand it. And therefore, whosoever wishes to find and to feel within himself those three unions of which I am going to speak, he must live entirely and wholly in God, so that he may satisfy and be amenable to the grace and the stirring of God, in all virtues and inward exercises.

And he must be lifted up through love, and die in God to himself and all his works; so that he yields himself up with all his powers, and submits to the transformation through the incomprehensible Truth which is God Himself. And to that end it is needful that living he should go forth in the virtues, and dying should enter into God. And in these two things his perfect life consists; and these two are joined together within him like matter and form, like body and soul. And as he exercises himself in them so he becomes clear in understanding, and rich and overflowing in feeling; for he has joined himself to God with uplifted powers, with true intention, with his heart's desire, with ceaseless craving, with the living ardour of his spirit and of his nature. And since he thus exercises himself and keeps himself in the Presence of God, love overpowers him: in whatsoever manner he moves, he is ever growing in love and in all virtues. But love always moves each man according to the profit and the ability of each.

CHAPTER VI

OF HEAVENLY WEAL AND HELLISH WOE

The most profitable stirrings which such a man can feel, and for which he is best fitted, are heavenly weal and hellish woe, and the ability to respond to these two with fit and proper works. For heavenly weal lifts a man up above all things into an untrammelled power of praising and loving God in every way that his heart and his soul desire. After this comes hellish woe, and casts him down into a misery, and into a lack of all the comfort and consolation that he experienced before. In this woe, weal sometimes shows itself, and brings with it a hope which none can gainsay. And then the man falls back again into a despair in which he can find no consolation.

When a man feels God within himself with rich and full grace, this I call heavenly health; for then he is wise and clear of understanding, rich and outflowing with heavenly teachings, ardent and generous in charity, drunken and overflowing with joy, strong in feeling, bold and ever ready in all the things which he knows to be well pleasing to God; and such-like things without number, which may only be known by those who feel them.

But when the scale of love goes down, and God hides Himself with all His graces, then the man falls back into dereliction and torment and dark misery, as though he should never more recover: and then he feels himself to be nought else but a poor sinner, who knows little or nothing of God.

He scorns every consolation that creatures may give him; and the taste and consolation of God he does not receive. And then his reason says within him: Where is now thy God? What hath become of all that thou didst receive from God? Then his tears are his meat day and night, as the Prophet says. Now if that man is to recover from this misery, he must observe and feel that he does not belong to himself, but to God; and therefore he must freely abandon his own will to the will of God, and must leave God to work in him in time and in eternity. So soon as he can do this, with untroubled heart, and with a free spirit, at that very moment he recovers his health, and brings heaven into hell, and hell into heaven.

For howsoever the scales of love go up and down, all things to him are even or alike. For whatsoever love gives or takes away, he who abandons himself and loves God finds peace in all. For his spirit remains free and unmoved, who lives in all pains without rebellion; and he is able to feel the unmediated union with God. For he has achieved the union through means by the richness of his virtues. And after this, because he is one aim and one will with God, he feels God within himself together with the fulness of His grace, as the quickening health of his being and all his works.

CHAPTER VII

SHOWING WHEREFORE ALL GOOD MEN DO NOT ATTAIN TO THE UNMEDIATED UNION WITH GOD

But now you may ask me why all good men do not attain to feel this. Now listen and I will tell you the why and the wherefore. They do not respond to the stirring of God with a forsaking of themselves, and so they do not abide with quickening fervour before the Presence of God; and also they are not careful of heart in their inward self-examination.

And therefore they always remain more outward and manifold than inward and simple, and they work their works more from good custom than from inward feeling. And they care more for particular methods and the greatness and multiplicity of good works than for the intention and love towards God. And so they remain outward and manifold of heart, and are not aware of how God lives in them with the fulness of grace.

CHAPTER VIII

SHOWING HOW THE INWARD MAN SHOULD EXERCISE HIMSELF, THAT HE MAY BE UNITED WITH GOD WITHOUT MEANS

But now I will tell you how the inward man, who has health amidst all miseries, should feel himself to be one with God without means. When such a quickened man rises up, with his whole being and all his powers, and joins himself to God with life-giving and active love, then he feels that his love is, in its ground, where it begins and ends, fruitive and without ground. If he then wishes to penetrate further, with his active love, into that fruitive love: then, all the powers of his soul must give way, and they must suffer and patiently endure that piercing Truth and Goodness which is God's self.

For, as the air is penetrated by the brightness and heat of the sun, and iron is penetrated by fire; so that it works through fire the works of fire, since it burns and shines like the fire; and so likewise it can be said of the air — for, if the air had understanding, it could say: "I enlighten and brighten the whole world" — yet each of these keeps its own nature. For the fire does not become iron, and the iron does not become fire, though their union is without means; for the iron is within the fire and the fire within the iron; and so also the air is in the sunshine and the sunshine in the air. So likewise is God in the being of the soul; and whenever the soul's highest powers are turned inward with active love, they are united with God without means, in a simple knowledge of all truth, and in an essential feeling and tasting of all good.

This simple knowing and feeling of God is possessed in essential love, and is practised and preserved through active love. And therefore it is accidental to our powers through the dying introversion in love; but it is essential to our being, and always abides within it. And therefore we must perpetually turn inwards and be renewed in love, if we would seek out love through love.

And this is taught us by St John, where he says: He that Dwelleth in Love Dwelleth in God and God in him. And though this union of the loving spirit with God is without means, yet there is here a great distinction, for the creature never becomes God, nor does God ever become the creature; as I explained to you heretofore in the example of the iron and the fire. And if material things, which have been made by God, may thus be united without means; so much the more may He, whenever such is His pleasure, unite Himself with His beloved, if they, through His grace, submit to it and make themselves ready for it. And so in such an inward man, whom God has adorned with virtues, and, above that, has lifted up into a contemplative life, there is no intermediary between himself and God in his highest introversion but his enlightened reason and his active love.

And through these two things, he has an adherence

to God; and this is "becoming one with God," says St Bernard. But above reason, and above active love, he is lifted up into a naked contemplation, and dwells without activity in essential love. And there he is one love and one spirit with God, as I said heretofore.

In this essential love, through the unity which he has essentially with God, he infinitely transcends his understanding; and this is a life common to all God-seeing men. For in this transcendence such a man is able to see in one sight — if it be God's pleasure to show it to him — all the creatures in heaven and on earth, with the distinction of their lives and their rewards. But before the Infinity of God, he must yield, and must follow after It essentially and without end; for This no creature, not even the soul of our Lord Jesus Christ, which yet received the highest union above all other creatures, can either comprehend or overtake.

CHAPTER IX

OF THE INWARD WORKING OF GOD'S GRACE

Behold, this Eternal Love, which lives within the spirit, and with which it is united without means, gives its light and its grace to all the powers of the soul; and becomes thereby the cause of all the virtues. For the grace of God touches the highest powers of the soul, and from this touch there spring charity and the knowledge of truth, the love of all righteousness, the practice of the counsels of God according to discretion, freedom from images, the overcoming of all things without effort, and the death into the Unity through love. As long as a man can maintain himself in this exercise, he is able to contemplate, and to feel the union without means; and he feels the touch of God within himself, which is a renewal of grace and all virtues.

You must further know that the grace of God also pours forth even through the lowest powers, and touches a man's heart; and from this there comes forth a heart-felt love towards God and a sensible joy in Him; and the love and delight pierce through heart and senses, through flesh and blood, and the whole bodily nature, and cause a pressure and restlessness in all his members, so that he is often at his wit's end. For he feels like a man full of wine, who is no longer master of himself.

And from this there come many a strange state, wherein men of tender heart cannot well govern themselves. Sometimes through impatient longing, they lift up their heads and gaze with wide-opened eyes towards heaven; now joying, now weeping; now singing, now crying; now in weal, now in woe, and often both together; running and jumping, laughing, clapping their hands, kneeling, bowing down: and many other like gestures are seen in them. So long as a man remains thus, and lifts himself up with an open heart towards those riches of God which live in his spirit, he feels ever anew the stirring of God, and the impatience of love; and then all these things are renewed in him.

And so this man through this bodily feeling may sometimes pass into a ghostly feeling which is according to reason; and through this ghostly feeling, he may pass into a godly feeling, which is above reason; and, through this godly feeling, he may drown himself in an unchangeable and beatific feeling. This feeling is our superessential blessedness, which is a fruition of God and all His beloved: and this blessedness is that Dark Quiet which ever abides in idleness. To God it is essential, and to all creatures superessential. And there we may behold how the Persons give place and abide in the Essential Love, that is, in the Fruitive Unity; and yet they dwell for ever, according to Their personal nature, in the working of the Trinity.

CHAPTER X

OF THE MUTUAL CONTENTMENT OF THE DIVINE PERSONS, AND THE MUTUAL CONTENTMENT BETWEEN GOD AND GOOD MEN

And so you may perceive that the Divine Nature eternally works according to the Persons, and is eternally idle and wayless according to the simplicity of Its Essence. All therefore that God has chosen and laid hold of with eternal personal love, has already been essentially and fruitively possessed of Him in unity with essential love. For the Divine Persons are enfolded within the Unity in a mutual embrace in an eternal contentment, in abysmal active love. And this is perpetually renewed in the life-giving life of the Trinity; for here there takes place a perpetual new birth in new knowledge new contentment and new outbreathing; in a new embrace, with new torrents of Eternal Love.

In this contentment all the chosen are enfolded: angels and men, from the first even to the last. Upon this contentment depend heaven and earth, and life, and being, and the activity and preservation of all creatures, save only the tendency to turn from God in sin: this comes from the wilful and blind wickedness of the creatures. From the Divine contentment grace and glory and all gifts pour forth in heaven and on earth, and into each creature separately, according to its needs and its receptivity. For God's grace is made ready for all men, and awaits the conversion of every sinner, and whenever a sinner, urged by grace, renounces himself and will call upon God with faith, he finds pardon.

And likewise, whosoever through grace with loving contentment turns towards the Eternal Contentment of God, he is enwrapped and embraced in the abysmal love which is God Himself.

And thereby he is perpetually renewed in love and in the virtues; for, between our contentment in God and God's contentment in us there abides an activity of love and of eternal life. But God has eternally loved us and established us within His contentment, and if we rightly observe this, our love and our contentment shall be wakened anew. For, in the mutual relations of the Persons in the Godhead, this contentment perpetually renews itself, in a new gushing forth of love, in an ever new embrace within the Unity. And this takes place beyond Time; that is, without before and after, in an eternal now.

For, in this embrace in the Unity, all things are consummated; and in the gushing forth of love, all things are wrought; and in the life-giving and fruitful Nature lie the power and possibilities of all things. For in the life-giving and fruitful Nature, the Son is in the Father, and the Father in the Son, and the Holy Ghost in Both.

For It is a life-giving and fruitful Unity, which is the home and the beginning of all life and of all becoming. And so all creatures are therein, beyond themselves, one Being and one Life with God, as in their Eternal Origin.

But in the precession of the different Persons, the Son proceeds from the Father, and the Holy Ghost from Both: and it is there that God has made and ordained all creatures according to their proper being, and has re-made man, through His grace and His death, inasmuch as he cleaves to Him. And He has adorned His own with love and with the virtues; and has turned back with them, towards His Origin.

There the Father and the Son and all the beloved are enfolded and embraced in the bonds of love; that is, in the unity of the Holy Ghost. And this is that same unity which is fruitful in the outgoing activity of the Persons, and forms in Their return an eternal bond of love which shall never be untied: and all who know themselves to be bound up in it shall be blessed throughout eternity, and they are rich in virtue, and clear in contemplation, and simple in fruitive rest. For in their introversion, the Love of God is revealed to them, pouring forth with all good, and drawing back again into the Unity, and above all being and beyond all conditions abiding in eternal rest. And so they are all united with God, through means, and without means, and also without distinction.

CHAPTER XI

HOW GOOD MEN IN THEIR CONTEMPLATION HAVE THE LOVE OF GOD BEFORE THEM, AND HOW THEY ARE LIFTED UP INTO GOD

They have the Love of God before them in their inward seeing, as a common good pouring forth through heaven and earth; and they feel the Holy Trinity inclined towards them, and within them, with fulness of grace. And therefore they are adorned without and within with all the virtues, with holy practices and with good works. And thus they are united with God through Divine grace and their own holy lives. And because they have abandoned themselves to God in doing, in leaving undone, and in suffering, they have steadfast peace and inward joy, consolation and savour, of which the world cannot partake; neither any dissembler, nor the man who seeks and means himself more than the glory of God.

Moreover, those same inward and enlightened men have before them in their inward seeing whenever they will, the Love of God as something drawing or urging them into the Unity; for they see and feel that the Father with the Son through the Holy Ghost, embrace Each Other and all the chosen, and draw themselves back with eternal love into the unity of Their Nature.

Thus the Unity is ever drawing to itself and inviting to itself every- thing that has been born of It, either by nature or by grace. And therefore, too, such enlightened men are, with a free spirit, lifted up above reason into a bare and imageless vision, wherein lives the eternal indrawing summons of the Divine Unity; and, with an imageless and bare understanding, they pass through all works, and all exercises, and all things, until they reach the summit of their spirits.

There, their bare understanding is drenched through by the Eternal Brightness, even as the air is drenched through by the sunshine. And the bare, uplifted will is transformed and drenched through by abysmal love, even as iron is by fire. And the bare, uplifted memory feels itself enwrapped and established in an abysmal Absence of Image. And thereby the created image is united above reason in a threefold way with its Eternal Image, which is the origin of its being and its life; and this origin is preserved and possessed, essentially and eternally, through a simple seeing in an imageless void: and so a man is lifted up above reason in a threefold manner into the Unity, and in a onefold manner into the Trinity.

Yet the creature does not become God, for the union takes place in God through grace and our homeward-turning love: and therefore the creature in its inward contemplation feels a distinction and an otherness between itself and God. And though the union is without means, yet the manifold works which God works in heaven and on earth are nevertheless hidden from the spirit. For though God gives Himself as He is, with clear discernment, He gives Himself in the essence of the soul, where the powers of the soul are simplified above reason, and where, in simplicity, they suffer the transformation of God. There all is full and overflowing, for the spirit feels itself to be one truth and one richness and one unity with God.

Yet even here there is an essential tending forward, and therein is an essential distinction between the being of the soul and the Being of God; and this is the highest and finest distinction which we are able to feel.

CHAPTER XII

OF THE HIGHEST UNION, WITHOUT DIFFERENCE OR DISTINCTION

And after this there follows the union without distinction. For you must apprehend the Love of God not only as an outpouring with all good, and as drawing back again into the Unity; but it is also, above all distinction, an essential fruition in the bare Essence of the Godhead. And in consequence of this, enlightened men have found within themselves an essential contemplation which is above reason and without reason, and a fruitive tendency which pierces through every condition and all being, and through which they immerse themselves in a wayless abyss of fathomless beatitude, where the Trinity of the Divine Persons possess Their Nature in the essential Unity.

Behold, this beatitude is so onefold and so wayless that in it every essential gazing, tendency, and creaturely distinction cease and pass away. For by this fruition, all uplifted spirits are melted and noughted in the Essence of God, Which is the superessence of all essence. There they fall from themselves into a solitude and an ignorance which are fathomless; there all light is turned to darkness; there the three Persons give place to the Essential Unity, and abide without distinction in fruition of essential blessedness. This blessedness is essential to God, and superessential to all creatures; for no created essence can become one with God's Essence and pass away from its own substance. For so the creature would become God, which is impossible; for the Divine Essence can neither wax nor wane, nor can anything be added to It or taken from It.

Yet all loving spirits are one fruition and one blessedness with God without distinction; for that beatific state, which is the fruition of God and of all His beloved, is so simple and onefold that therein neither Father, nor Son, nor Holy Ghost, is distinct according to the Persons, neither is any creature. But all enlightened spirits are here lifted up above themselves into a wayless fruition, which is an abundance beyond all the fulness that any creature has ever received or shall ever receive. For there all uplifted spirits are, in their superessence, one fruition and one beatitude with God without distinction; and there this beatitude is so onefold that no distinction can enter into it.

And this was prayed for by Christ when He besought His Father in heaven that all His beloved might be made perfect in one, even as He is one with the Father through the Holy Ghost: even so He prayed and besought that He in us and we in Him and His heavenly Father might be one in fruition through the Holy Ghost. And this I think the most loving prayer which Christ ever made for our blessedness.

CHAPTER XIII

OF THE THREEFOLD PRAYER OF CHRIST, THAT WE MIGHT BE ONE WITH GOD

But you should also observe that His prayer, as it has been written by St John in this same Gospel, was threefold. For He prayed that we might be with Him, that we might behold the glory which His Father had given Him. And therefore I said at the beginning that all good men are united with God by means of Divine grace and their own virtuous life; for the love of God is always pouring into us with new gifts, and whosoever is aware of this is fulfilled with new virtues and holy exercises and with all good, in the way that I told you heretofore: and this union through the fulness of grace and glory, in body and soul, begins here below and shall endure throughout eternity.

Further, Christ prayed thus, that He might be in us and we in Him. This we find in the Gospel, in many places. And this is the union without means; for the Love of God is not only outpouring, but it also draws us inwards, into the Unity. And those who feel and are aware of this, become inward and enlightened men, and their highest powers are uplifted, above all exercises, into their naked being: and there, above reason, the powers become simplified in their essence, and so they are full and overflowing. For in that simplicity, the spirit finds itself united with God without means; and this union, with the exercise which belongs to it, shall endure eternally, as I have told you heretofore.

Further, Christ uttered His most sublime prayer, namely, that His beloved might be made perfect in one, as He is one with the Father: not one as He is with the Father one single Divine Substance, for this is impossible to us; but so one, and in such a unity, as He is one fruition and one beatitude with the Father without distinction in Essential Love. Those who are thus united with God in this threefold way, in them the prayer of Christ has been fulfilled.

These with God shall ebb and flow,

Having and joying, they shall empty go;

They shall both work and passively endure,

And in their superessence rest secure.

They shall go out and in, and find their food,

And, drunk with love, in radiant darkness sleep in God.

Many more words I should like to say here, but those who possess this have no need of them: and he to whom it has been shown, and who cleaves with love to Love, he shall be taught the whole truth by Love itself. But those who turn outwards, and would find consolation in outward things, do not feel this;

and, even though I should say much more of it, yet they would not understand. For those who give themselves wholly to outward works, or those who are idle in inward passivity, shall never be able to understand it.

Now although reason and all bodily feelings must here give place and yield to the faith and contemplation of the spirit, and to those things which are above reason; yet reason and also the life of the senses continue to abide in their place, and cannot pass away, any more than the nature of man can pass away. And further, though the gazing and tendency of the spirit towards God must give place to fruition in simplicity; yet this gazing and this tendency continue to exist in their place. For this is the inmost life of the spirit; and, in the enlightened and uplifted man, the life of the senses adheres to the spirit. And so his sensual powers are joined to God by heart-felt love, and his nature is fulfilled with all good; and he feels that his ghostly life adheres to God without means. And thereby his highest powers are uplifted to God in eternal love, and drenched through by Divine truth, and established in imageless freedom. And so he is filled with God, and overflowing without measure.

In this inundation there comes to pass the essential outpouring or immersion in the superessential Unity; and this is the union without distinction, of which I have often told you. For in the superessence all our \says end. If we will go with God upon the highway of love, we shall rest with Him eternally and without end: and thus we shall eternally go forth towards God and enter into Him and rest in Him.

CHAPTER XIV

HERE THE AUTHOR DECLARES THAT HE SUBMITS ALL THAT HE HAS WRITTEN TO THE JUDGMENT OF HOLY CHURCH

Now at this time I cannot set forth my meaning more clearly. In all that I understand, or feel, or have written, I submit myself to the judgment of the saints and of Holy Church; for I wish to live and to die as a servant of Christ, in the Christian faith; and I desire to be, by the grace of God, a life-giving member of Holy Church. And therefore, as I told you heretofore, you should beware of those self-deceived men who, by means of their idle vacancy, and with their bare and simple gaze have found the Divine Essence within themselves in a merely natural way; and who pretend to be one with God without the grace of God, and without exercise of virtue, and without obedience to God and to Holy Church. And for all their perversity of life, which I have described, they would be one with God's Son by nature. But if the Prince of all the angels was cast out of heaven, because he set himself up against God and would be like unto the most High; and if the first man was driven from Paradise because he would be as God: how then shall this wretched sinner — that is, the faithless Christian who would be as God without likeness to God in grace and virtue — ever rise from earth into heaven?

For through his own power no man has ascended into heaven, save the Son of Man, Jesus Christ. And therefore we must unite ourselves with Him, through grace and virtue and Christian faith: so we shall ascend with Him whither He has gone before us. For in the Last Day we shall all rise, each with his own body; and then those who have worked good works shall go into life everlasting, and those who have worked evil works shall go into everlasting fire. These are two unlike ends, which shall never come together; for each flies from the other perpetually.

Pray for him who has composed and written this, that God may have mercy upon him. That his poor beginning, and his and our wretched middle course, may be brought to a blessed end, this may Jesus Christ, the Son of the living God, bestow upon us all.

AMEN.

ABOUT THE PUBLISHER

Azafran Books was established with a clear aim in mind – to make available a selection of classic books for today's contemporary readers. The books in our catalogue have been selected from a broad range of themes: such as philosophy (occidental & oriental), mysticism & magic, new thought, religion & spirituality, folktales, mythology, cult fiction, poetry, social commentary and psychology. Yet they all have a common theme, or purpose – to stimulate our thinking and modes of perception. For this reason, they have been chosen to be re-published and re-presented to the modern reader.

Most of the books published by us are currently out of copyright, and may be found as digital files in the public domain. We make no disguise of this fact. And if you wish to glance at a digital copy, perhaps for curiosity sake, then we may suggest that you find a free copy to download from the internet. We, at Azafran Books, prefer to offer a service in presenting these books in a new, updated format, as modern, well-designed and pleasing paperbacks. It is our intention that the books we publish are pleasing to the eye as well as a pleasure to read. Many of the re-published books in our catalogue will have specially written introductions or forwards, in order to introduce the new reader to the material. Moreover, each new edition has been carefully edited and formatted to the highest of standards – by a 'real person' and not by a computer program! In this way, we hope to offer a service. For those readers who would prefer to spend a little money to buy an affordable book, we make efforts to place a pleasantly designed copy in your hands at not much more cost that the price of printing a copy yourself from a digital file.

Our aim at Azafran Books is to bring a range of stimulating books, many of them largely forgotten, to the attention of the reader today. In other words, to bring you 'Classic Books for a Contemporary World.'

Please visit us at - www.azafranbooks.com

AZAFRAN BOOK CATALOGUE

THE ALCHEMY OF HAPPINESS – Al-Ghazzali

THE CLOUD UPON THE SANCTUARY – Karl Von Eckartshausen

JEWISH MYSTICISM - J. Abelson

SONGS OF KABIR – Rabindranath Tagore

BUSHIDO: THE SOUL OF JAPAN – Inazo Nitobe

THE COMTE DE ST. GERMAIN - Isabel Cooper-Oakley

THE LIFE OF THE BEE – Maurice Maeterlinck

JESUS, THE LAST GREAT INITIATE – Edouard Schure

THE KASÎDAH – Sir Richard Burton

ON FRIENDSHIP & LOVE - Edward Carpenter

ON CULTURE & SOCIETY - Edward Carpenter

LOOKING BACKWARD - Edward Bellamy

THE STORY OF UTOPIAS - Lewis Mumford

MYTH OF THE BIRTH OF THE HERO - Otto Rank

LEGENDS OF THE SUFIS – El Eflaki

THE BOOK OF THE LOVER – Ramon Llull

FOUNTAIN OF LIFE (FONS VITAE) – Solomon Ibn Gabirol

TIBETAN FOLK TALES

DIVINE NAMES - Dionysius

HAYY IBN YAQZAN – Ibn Tufail

SELECTED WORKS - John of Ruusbroec

Printed in Great Britain
by Amazon

58907178R00078